THROUGH FIFTY YEARS

THROUGH FIFTY YEARS

A HISTORY OF
THE SURMA VALLEY LIGHT HORSE

BY

THE REV. W. H. S. WOOD, M.C.,
Honorary Chaplain to the Forces
and
Chaplain to the Surma
Valley Light Horse.

The Naval & Military Press Ltd

Published by
The Naval & Military Press Ltd
5 Riverside, Brambleside, Bellbrook
Industrial Estate, Uckfield, East Sussex,
TN22 1QQ England
Tel: +44 (0) 1825 749494
Fax: +44 (0) 1825 765701
www.naval-military-press.com
www.military-genealogy.com

In reprinting in facsimile from the original, any imperfections are inevitably reproduced and the quality may fall short of modern type and cartographic standards.

Lt-Col. Milne and the Officers of the Surma Valley Light Horse 1888.

FOREWORD

TO the thousands of men who have, at any time, been resident in North Eastern India, especially to those who have been connected with the Tea Industry in the Surma Valley, the history of the Surma Valley Light Horse will make most excellent reading. To those whose association with the district goes back to thirty or forty years, the names of such stalwarts as Showers, MacLaughlin, Pat Chamney, and others, will conjure up happy memories of long treks over bad roads and across country, with no roads at all, to attend parades; of doughty deeds of tent-pegging, lime-cutting, and jumping, and of sincere good fellowship after the day's work was done. We have all heard the old stagers saying:—
"Ah, those were the days, me boys, when we rode twenty or thirty miles to parades and rode all the way back again! Can't do it now. Have to get wheeled in a Ford car or something!" But, I fancy, if a car had been going in those good old days, they would not have been so keen on the long *daks*!

Conditions have changed, but, thank God, the lads are just the same old type and will turn up trumps whenever called upon to do so.

The history of the Surma Valley Light Horse is a record of progress and achievement in the district from the time when it was opened out from virgin jungle to the present day.

We are all greatly indebted to the author for the tremendous amount of research work he has undertaken in hunting up old records which we all thought were long lost and forgotten.

J. MACKNIGHT, LIEUT.-COL.,
Commandant, Surma Valley Light Horse.

PREFACE.

I HAVE been prompted to write this history through the realisation that a great deal of the events that have occurred in the Surma Valley have disappeared into oblivion. It has been my privilege to unearth some of the history of Tea in Cachar and Sylhet from the Record Books, and, basing my effort on a *Short History of the Surma Valley Light Horse*, written by Captain E. E. Dyball in the Annual Report of the Regiment for 1919-20, I have been able to give some idea of the progress of the Corps through fifty years of its existence, beginning with the Sylhet Volunteer Rifle Corps, which was started in 1880, and of which, unfortunately, practically nothing is known, down to 1930, when Colours were presented to the Surma Valley Light Horse.

There is no claim that this history is complete, but it is complete so far as it goes. What it needs are those personal touches, little anecdotes and incidents, which can only be provided by those who have a far better knowledge of the Regiment than I have, and it may be that a future historian will combine these with the statement of facts which has been gathered for the most part from the Annual Reports, which have been placed at my disposal by the Commandant of the Regiment.

The Chapter on the South African War could not have been written without the very considerable help I received from Lieut.-Col. H. Chamney, C.M.G., and Mrs. V. E. Bigge. To the former I am indebted for most of the photographs that appear in this history and for the loan of letters and newspaper cuttings relating to the South African War. Mrs. Bigge had kept a complete newspaper file of the events of Lumsden's Horse, and not only allowed me to use these, but was good enough to arrange them in order. I wish to offer Colonel Chamney and Mrs. Bigge my grateful thanks for their help.

I would also wish to express my thanks to the Deputy Commissioners of Cachar who gave me permission to search the Record Books of Cachar.

Many others have helped by their suggestions and by the loan of photographs, in fact the whole history is the result of that co-operation which we, in the Surma Valley Light Horse, know so well.

I am especially indebted to my friends, Mr. G. E. Parker, and Mr. L. E. Boothroyd for their kindness in seeing the book through the press.

In conclusion, I wish to dedicate this book to all those who have been, are, and will be, members of the Surma Valley Light Horse.

W. H. S. WOOD.

June, 1930

Non-Commissioned Officers
1888.

CONTENTS.

	PAGE.
FOREWORD BY LIEUT.-COL. J. MACKNIGHT	v
PREFACE	vii
LIST OF ILLUSTRATIONS	xi
THE BEGINNINGS OF THE VOLUNTEER MOVEMENT IN THE SURMA VALLEY	1
THE SURMA VALLEY LIGHT HORSE, 1886, TO THE MANIPUR CAMPAIGN	13
THE MANIPUR CAMPAIGN, 1891	17
FROM 1892 TO THE SOUTH AFRICAN WAR	26
THE SOUTH AFRICAN WAR	32
1901-1914	45
THE END OF THE VOLUNTEERS, 1915-1917	57
THE INDIAN DEFENCE FORCE	60
THE AUXILIARY FORCE INDIA, 1921-1929	66
THE FIFTIETH YEAR, 1930	72
APPENDIX I. ROLL OF OFFICERS	81
APPENDIX II. ROLL OF STAFF	84
APPENDIX III. ROLL OF INSTRUCTIONAL STAFF	85
APPENDIX IV. DECORATIONS AND AWARDS GAINED BY MEMBERS OF THE CORPS	87

LIST OF ILLUSTRATIONS.

Lieut.-Col. Milne and the Officers of the Surma Valley Light Horse, 1888	*Facing*	*Foreword.*
Non-Commissioned Officers, 1888.	,,	*Contents.*
Two Sergeants, S. V. L. H., 1892.	,,	*Page* 1.
Lieut.-Col J. Knox-Wight	,,	,, 2.
Remainder of the Men who served in the Manipur Campaign, 1891, at Karimganj, 1897.	,,	,, 9
Karimganj Camp, 1896. Regiment in Quarter Column.	,,	,, 13
S. V. L. H., Karimganj Camp, 1896. Officers' Sword Exercise.	,,	,, 17
Officers. 1897.	,,	,, 20
"B" Company, Lumsden's Horse Contingent, South African War, 1900.	,,	,, 31
"B" Company Lumsden's Horse. Departure from Calcutta for South African War, 1900	,,	,, 32
Lieut-Col. E. C. Showers, 1895-1899	,,	,, 34
Funeral of Colonel Showers in South Africa. 1900	,,	,, 39
The Salute to Colonel Showers, South Africa, 1900	,,	,, 39
Lieut-Col. A. J. M. MacLaughlin, C.I.E. 1900-1907	,,	,, 40
Boers, 1900	,,	,, 42
Fording a River : The S. V.L.H. South Africa, 1900.	,,	,, 42

LIST OF ILLUSTRATIONS—*Contd.*

"Good-bye, Brother Boer," South Africa 1900 ...	*Facing Page*	44
Surma Valley Light Horse Leaving South Africa, 1900.	,, ,,	44
Leaving Cape Town. Homeward Bound, 1900 ...	,, ,,	44
Lieut-Col. Richard Wood 1907-1911	,, ,,	46
Lieut-Col. W. R. Walker, Second in Command and sometime Acting-Commandant, 1908. ...	,, ,,	50
Lieut-Col. J. G. Knowles, C.I.E., 1911-1919 ...	,, ,,	54
Lieut-Col. R. St. J. Hickman, C.I.E. 1919-1924 ...	,, ,,	58
Lieut-Col. H. D. Marshall, C.I.E., O.B.E., 1924-1927	,, ,,	62
Lieut-Col. J. Macknight, 1927-1930	,, ,,	66
Lieut-Col. A. B. Beddow, 1930	,, ,,	70
Consecration of the Guidon. February 1930 ...	,, ,,	72
Presentation of the Guidon. February 1930 ...	,, ,,	72
Officers, Surma Valley Light Horse 1930, with Major-General H. E. ap Rhys Price, G. O. C., Presidency and Assam. ... — ...	,, ,,	75
Detachment at Chittagong 1930 ...	,, ,,	77
Surma Valley Light Horse Camp, 1930 ...	,, ,,	79

Two Sergeants S. V. L. H. 1892.

CHAPTER I.

THE BEGINNINGS OF THE VOLUNTEER MOVEMENT IN THE SURMA VALLEY.

THE Surma Valley Light Horse, as such, came into existence in 1886; but there were several movements towards the establishment of a military unit or units before this which date back to 1857, two years after Tea was discovered in Cachar.

The first notice of any member of the Planting Community in the Surma Valley volunteering and taking part in active service occurs during the Indian Mutiny of 1857. In a letter of the 7th December of that year, Captain R. Stewart, the Superintendent of Cachar, reports that three companies of the 34th Native Infantry stationed at Chittagong had mutinied and were marching north. On the 18th there was an engagement at Latu, in Sylhet, between the mutineers and the Sylhet Light Infantry, commanded by Major Byng, and the former were completely routed and fled into Cachar where a few small engagements occurred. The mutineers were completely dispersed in June, 1858.

During this time several planters volunteered their services and in the Cachar Record Books a letter appears, dated 2nd January, 1858, which gives an idea of the work which they undertook. " They (the mutineers) were tracked up by Kookie Scouts . . . . . . these scouts were men of a Kookie village in the lands of the Cachar Tea Company, supplied by me with firearms, and I beg to bring to your Honor's favourable notice the conduct of Mr. James Davidson, the manager of that Company, who directed them and who, during the five days that the mutineers were wandering in the wilderness, kept me continually supplied with excellent and reliable information concerning their movements."

Six planters were awarded the Mutiny Medal—Messrs. J. Davidson, J. Boothby, J. Sandeman, A. Tydd, A. Brownlow and H. A. Brownlow, and the medal was accompanied by the following letter:— " It is with great pleasure that I do myself the honor to forward you the accompanying medal granted to you by Her Most Gracious Majesty the Queen for your services in Cachar during the Mutiny."

This, of course, has no direct bearing on the history that follows, but it indicates that the ground was in course of preparation for the Volunteer movement. Two years later, when Captain Stewart was trying to recover the muskets lent during the Mutiny, there is a suspicion that some sort of volunteer movement has been hinted at, for in reply to a letter he mentions that " the muskets were not given to you . . . . . . for any volunteering purposes."

The first real suggestion occurs in a letter dated the 9th May, 1862. "In his recent visit to Cachar, Brig.-General Showers, Commanding the Presidency Division and deputed specially to this Frontier to settle existing disturbances, called my attention to the possibility of forming a Volunteer Rifle Corps in Cachar from among the European residents as one of the most likely measures to insure future peace and quietness in the District and prevent internal disturbances. The General assures me of his hearty co-operation in any such movement and promised to assist it by the deputation of competent drill instructors, as well as with the supply of arms from Government Stores. I have, therefore, now the honor to call upon such as are willing to form a disciplined body to subscribe their names. It will be necessary for subscribers to attend periodically at drills either at the Station or at rendezvous duly appointed so as to suit their convenience. The terms of this attendance, as well as the election of officers, etc., will be arranged at a general meeting of subscribers when their number shall have been ascertained. Trusting that you will see the expediency and desirability of perfecting the measure proposed."

It is not until 1865 that we hear of the movement again. On the 23rd May, Captain Stewart writes to a firm of military tailors as follows :—" I shall be obliged by your informing me at what rate you will be able to let me have, say, one hundred Elwood helmets of a uniform shape, and two hundred American drill khaki coloured

LIEUT-COL. J. KNOX-WIGHT.
1883-1887.

BEGINNINGS OF THE VOLUNTEER MOVEMENT

tunics for a Corps of Volunteers about to be started in Cachar. The helmet for privates is to be plain, with a khaki turban for corporals, sergeants and officers, to be ornamented according to rank, and the tunics likewise."

On the same date letters are addressed to the Commandant, Calcutta Volunteers, Calcutta, and to the Commandant, Punjab Volunteer Rifle Corps, Lahore. "I shall feel very much obliged to you if you will be so good as to let me have a copy of the rules and regulations and bye-laws of the Corps of Volunteers under your command. A Volunteer force is about to be raised in Cachar and we would wish as much as possible to benefit by the experience of those who have gone before us. I need not say with what pleasure I shall receive any remarks that you yourself may have to offer on the subject of raising such a Corps. It is to be a mounted force and will consist, I hope, of about one hundred members."

On the 6th June, Captain Stewart sends the following letter to eighty-eight planters in Cachar. "You are hereby informed that a meeting of the members who have enrolled themselves to serve in the Cachar Mounted Volunteers will be held in the "Retreat Bungalow" on Monday the 19th inst., at 2 p.m. Your presence at the meeting is desired, but should you be unable to attend personally, pray be so good as to fill in and sign the accompanying paper authorising any one whom you know will be at the meeting to vote for you on the several questions which will be mooted." The "accompanying paper" is :—"I hereby authorise . . . . . . to vote for me at the Meeting of the Members of the Cachar Mounted Volunteers to be held on Monday the 19th June, 1865."

As a result of this meeting, of which, unfortunately, there appears to be no record, two further letters are sent out by Stewart. On the 21st June he writes to Dr. Coulter—"I send you the first copy of the proceedings of the Volunteers' Meeting that I have been able to get copied out, and must ask you to be good enough, with regard to the Hailakandy meeting that is to take place, to let your bungalow be made use of for the purpose. As soon as I have your consent to this proposal I shall fix a day for the meeting and Irvine and myself will be down to attend it. I only hope that it will go off as well as the meeting here which was very succesful. We have now 57 troopers in the Station Troop, besides officers and non-commissioned officers. I send you a list of the Hailakandy members as far as I have them enrolled, but am sorry not to see your own name amongst them, and hope you will put it down and get as many others as you can to join."

Another letter is written on the 22nd June to "My dear Irvine"—"I send you the nominal roll of the Station Troop with residence and distance of each member from Headquarters as correctly as I can supply it. Please fill it up by getting further information and correct it where it is wrong. Also please get from every member, through Phillips or by yourself, his measure according to the system of Harman and Co., which you will get from any of their books. I also send you a full copy of the proceedings of the two meetings, with the list of enrolled members, which please try and augment.

"*P.S.* I have written to Coulter proposing that a meeting should be held at his house of the Hailakandy members, and as soon as I hear from him I shall fix a day and summon the meeting, at which I should like both you and myself to be present."

Now, here we have a Volunteer Corps formed and ready to act; but, although the Cachar Record Books have been searched, no further reference is to be found, and we must assume that for some reason or another it failed to function.

The next effort occurs fifteen years later when the Sylhet Volunteer Rifle Corps was formed on the 22nd October, 1880. This was an infantry unit, for on the 30th March, 1885, Major Nicolay, who inspected the Sylhet Section of the Cachar and Sylhet Mounted Rifles, reports that "Sergt.-Inst. Cockshot is an infantryman and has applied for a transfer since the constitution of this one has been altered." Here again, we are unable to obtain any information, and not even the name of the Commanding Officer is known.

The Cachar Mounted Rifles was formed on the 6th April, 1883, and in the first Annual Report the Rules of "The Cachar Mounted Volunteer Rifle Corps" are published.

1. The members are subject to the provisions of Act XX of 1869 (an Act to provide for the good order and discipline of Volunteer Corps, and to invest them with certain powers), and of any other Act by which that Act shall be amended, to the Indian Volunteer Regulations, and to any orders which may be issued by competent authority.

2. The Corps shall consist of two classes :—
   a. Enrolled members, consisting of Efficients and Non-efficients.
   b. Honorary members, contributing to the funds of the corps, but not being enrolled for service.

3. The subscription shall be paid before the 1st January each year.

4. The annual subscription of members of the corps shall be Rs. 10 (ten), first year, Rs. 5 (five), second year.

5. No person shall be admitted as a member of the corps unless with the final approval of the Commandant.

6. Each member must be provided with uniform of the pattern selected by the corps and approved by the Local Government.

7. Each member shall be responsible for the due preservation of all articles issued to him which are the property of Her Majesty's Government or of the corps—fair wear and tear only excepted.

8. The expression "property of the corps" shall include all articles which have been purchased out of the general funds or presented to the corps.

9. When the corps is not assembled for actual service, the Commanding Officer is, by the general provisions of Act XX of 1869, solely responsible for the discipline of the Corps; but he may at any time assemble a Court of Enquiry, consisting of three or five members of the Corps (one of whom shall be an officer), to be appointed by roster, for the purpose of investigating any irregularity and assisting him in coming to a conclusion upon it. Any enquiry

in reference to a Commissioned Officer shall be made by a Court composed of Officers within the Province, convened under the authority of the Local Government.

10. The C.O. and Committee shall fix the time and place for parades, drills and rifle practice.

11. The Senior Officer in command shall have power, subject to the approval of the Commanding Officer, to inflict the following fines:—

> For loading contrary to order and shooting out of turn . . . . . . Rs. 2. For discharging the rifle accidentally . . . . . . Rs. 2. For pointing the same without orders, loaded or unloaded at any person, etc. . . . . . . Rs. 20.

12. All fines imposed on members of the corps shall be entered in a book kept by the Local Committee for that purpose.

13. All fines shall become due on the first day of every month succeeding that in which they have been inflicted, and shall be collected by the Local Committee.

14. The Commandant shall cause an abstract of the accounts to be annually prepared, and printed for the information of every member of the corps. The disposal of the capitation grants received from Government shall be shown separately from that of the corps subscriptions.

15. Honorary members may, if they wish it, wear the uniform of the Corps, but they are not to interfere in any way with its military duties.

16. Honorary members will be permitted to use the practice-ground when it is not required by the enrolled members.

17. Honorary members shall pay an annual subscription of Rs. 10.

18. The rules to be printed and copies distributed to members at Re.1 per copy.

19. The uniform shall be:—

> (a) Ankle boots and spurs.
> (b) Gaiters.

(c) Pants.
(d) Tunic.
(e) Sola helmet.
(f) Helmet lines.

The cost of the uniform will be approximately—

	Rs.	As.	P.
Tunic, Pants or Breeches	6	8	0
Gaiters	3	0	0
Helmet, spike and chain	4	0	0
Helmet lines	2	8	0
Total Rs	16	0	0

20. These rules may be added to, or amended, subject to the approval of a committee called by the Commanding Officer of not less than fifteen members, seven clear days' notice being given, and the nature of the proposed alterations being specified in such notice.

Major John Knox-Wight, the Deputy Commissioner of Cachar, was the first Commanding Officer, and by the end of the first year there were one hundred and fifty-three members of the Corps, including the staff. The Regiment was divided into two troops :—
A. The Hailakandy and Chutla Bheel Troop; B. The North Cachar, Lakhipur and Happy Valley Troop. Captain A. Milne commanded "A" Troop with Lieut. D. A. Laing as his second-in-command, and Captain S. D. Jackson commanded "B" troop assisted by Lieut. A. Stewart. Lieut. Ernest Livermore was Adjutant, Dr. A. J. M. MacLaughlin, Surgeon, and the Rev. T. T. Crossfield was Chaplain. On the 8th September, Troop Sergt.-Major R. Leigh, 11th Hussars, joined as Sergt.-Instructor, and on the 6th of May, 1884, Sergt. S. Roberts, 9th Lancers, reported for duty.

The first inspection was held at Silchar on the 29th March, 1884, and the Memorandum of remarks by the Inspecting Officer, Colonel H. A. Little, Commanding at Cachar, makes interesting reading:—

Manual and Firing Exercises. Were performed very fairly but several motions were rather too hurried and not marked by a pause of quick time between each.

Marching Past. Very well performed, the dressing being well kept and the men steady. In some few instances the carbine not correctly held at the carry, the toe of the butt pointing downwards, instead of the butt-plate being placed across the hollow of the thigh, toe to the left, barrel to the right.

Saluting. The officers' salute was not correctly performed either mounted or dismounted, the hand being kept in front of the body instead of being carried below the thigh at the full extent of the arm.

Arms. The rifles were generally in good order, with the exception of two or three which had not been wiped out the previous day, and several cleaning rods require burnishing.

Musketry. The rifles should be kept in the highest condition as otherwise it is impossible to produce good shooting with them. The practice very good, but the position when firing, both standing and lying down, not in accordance with regulations.

The Officers and Non-Commissioned Officers are well acquainted with their duties and the men steady in the ranks, considering the short period the Corps has been training and the few opportunities the men have had of being instructed, owing to the long distances which intervene between the different places for drill. Parade movements are, however, executed with wonderful steadiness, though " extending for skirmishing " and " mounting and retiring " should be done with greater rapidity.

The rapid progress which the Corps has made is very creditable to all concerned, and the evident desire of every individual member of it to make himself efficient should be encouraged, and the advantages which would result both to themselves and to the State from their praiseworthy exertion should be constantly borne in mind."

Drills had begun in December, 1883, and this report shows how keenly the first members threw themselves into the work. The Commanding Officer reports that out of one hundred and five members who " received some drills," twenty-three qualified as extra-efficients and thirty-four as efficients.

Early in March, 1884, the Commandant of the Sylhet Volunteer Rifle Corps wrote and suggested that the two units should combine.

Remainder of the Men who served in the Manipur Campaign 1891, at Karimganj Camp 1897

BEGINNINGS OF THE VOLUNTEER MOVEMENT

A meeting of the officers of the Cachar Mounted Rifles decided that it would be beneficial if two hundred and forty members could be obtained and the services of a paid adjutant could be secured. The proposals were accepted by both Corps and all details for carrying out the amalgamation were arranged and, from the 26th September, 1884, the Cachar and Sylhet Mounted Rifles came into existence. Three squadrons were formed of two troops each :—

    First Squadron ;   "A"   (Hailakandi and Chutla Bheel) and
                                "B"   (Happy Valley and Lakhipur)
    Second Squadron ; "C"   (North and North-West Cachar) and
                                "D"   (Chargola, Longai and Loobah)
    Third Squadron ;   "E"   (Lungla) and
                                "F"   (South Sylhet)

Major Knox-Wight was promoted to Lieut.-Col. and Captain A. Milne to Major.

In the Introduction to the Annual Report of the Cachar and Sylhet Mounted Rifles for 1884-85, the Commandant remarks :—
"While it is to be regretted that during the year under report the Corps did not learn much new drill, it is satisfactory to find that steps were taken in the majority of local centres to hold small parades at which both officers and men were exercised in such knowledge as they had acquired. While congratulating the Volunteers on their zeal in this respect, the Commandant would urge on all officers and non-commissioned officers the necessity of making themselves thoroughly acquainted with every detail of drill, so as to be able to hold these local parades independently of all instructors, whose visits must necessarily be few and far between ; and he further trusts that no trooper will wilfully fail to avail himself of the opportunities of instruction thus offered. When the Adjutant and Sergeant Instructors can be present it is still more incumbent on all ranks to attend.

The shooting during the past year was moderately good, considering that a large proportion of members fired for the first time with the Martini-Henry carbines, but the Commandant trusts that patience and perseverance will in no case be relaxed, and that the coming year will give the Corps a far higher figure of merit than has yet been obtained.

It is a matter of sincere congratulation that the Cachar and Sylhet Mounted Rifles are now amalgamated into one Corps consisting of three squadrons, for although it is seldom that the whole Regiment is likely to meet for parade and drill, still Cachar and Sylhet will feel that they are comrades in arms, and work in each others' interests accordingly."

Two inspections were held during that season, one in Silchar on the 28th February, 1885, when the Inspecting Officer was Colonel R. S. Robertson, 4th Bengal Infantry, and the second at Lungla on the 14th March, by Major F. W. Nicolay of the same Regiment. In both cases the parades were reported favourably upon, but one note is worthy of mention:—

"The Inspecting Officer had occasion, however, to draw attention to the unnecessary amount of talking that went on in the ranks during the parade. This grave fault is so easily corrected that it is hoped that it may never recur."

Major-Gen. T. D. B. Baker, Adjutant-General in India, in his report to the Secretary to the Government of India, Military Department, dated 24th June, 1885, writes:—

"In forwarding the Annual Inspection Report on the Cachar and Sylhet Mounted Rifles, dated 28th February and 14th March, 1885, I am directed to state that the Commander-in-Chief considers it to be altogether rather favourable, taking into consideration the short time that the Corps has been in existence; and that credit is due for the zeal displayed by the members and for the state of the arms, as well as for progress in drill."

In Colonel Robertson's report, he states:—"On the day previous to the inspection I had an opportunity of seeing a portion of the troops taking part in Field Manœuvres where they acquitted themselves very creditably and performed the duties of skirmishing and scouting with much intelligence. On the morning of the 28th I examined the officers in Troop Drill, of which they showed a fair knowledge. I then selected ten men indiscriminately from the ranks for target practice, which was performed in my presence under the superintendency of their own officers, who evinced a competent knowledge of Musketry Regulations. The shooting at 200 and 500 yards was very fair. In the evening the corps paraded for inspection; they were drawn up in two squadrons in single rank; they marched past by squadrons at the walk and trot; ranked past by single file and cantered past by squadrons. After this a few simple manœuvres were performed, terminating with the Carbine and Sword exercises. The march past, considering that this was the first time it had been done by squadrons, was very good, the men keeping well together, and the few battalion movements were fairly well done . . . . . .

In conclusion, I have much pleasure in stating that these two troops consist of a fine body of men . . . . . . as a rule well mounted on serviceable ponies, and good riders. I observed that they took a good deal of interest in their work and appeared very anxious to become proficient in their drill and duties generally. They labour under great disadvantages, as owing to the members of the Corps being scattered throughout the District, they have few opportunities of working together, but they seem full of zeal, and with a little more training and encouragement will, I am convinced, become a highly efficient and useful body of men."

Major Nicolay speaks similarly of the Sylhet Squadron.—" It is very creditable to report that many of those present on parade had ridden long distances to attend—some over thirty miles . . . . The majority of the gentlemen forming this Corps are Tea Planters in the District, generally speaking, good riders and very fair shots, well acquainted with the roads and paths about the country, and in case of being called upon would render excellent service in time of need to Government."

During that year, Lieut. A. Hutton, Madras S.C., Wing Officer and Adjutant, 1st Infantry, Hyderabad Contingent, was appointed as Adjutant; both Sergeant-Instructors rejoined their Regiments and 1st Class Sergt.-Inst. A. Kearney, 17th D. C. O. Lancers, became senior instructor, and three others—Sergt.-Major W. Haste, 12th Lancers, Sergt.-Major A. Lawrence, 17th Lancers, and Sergt.-Major R. Slater, 14th Hussars, also joined.

In February, 1886, the first Camps of Exercise were held, one at Silchar and the other at Kannyhatti. The Inspecting Officer was Lieut.-Col. H. E. Elliot, 4th Bengal Infantry, who, in his confidential report, writes:—

"The Cachar and Sylhet Mounted Rifle Volunteer Corps turned out for the inspection parades held by me at Silchar and Kannyhatti in very good numbers, when it is taken into consideration the long distances many have to travel—more especially in Sylhet—and the fact that in a garden where there are only two Europeans, not more than one is allowed to be absent at the same time. They appear to be an exceptionally fine body of Officers and men. Their physique is excellent, and the energy and enthusiasm which they have this year displayed in undergoing the realities of camp life and its many duties in the Camp of Exercise held at Silchar and Kannyhatti reflects the greatest credit on the Corps . . . . . . The Officers and men were well mounted and turned out smart and clean and, considering the few opportunities the Corps has of drilling together, the horses were remarkably steady."

In a letter addressed to the Chief Commissioner of Assam, we read:—" The Government of India concurs with His Excellency the Commander-in-Chief in considering the report to be satisfactory and is pleased to notice the remarks of the Inspecting Officer regarding the energy and enthusiasm displayed by this fine body of volunteers."

Karimganj Camp 1896
Regiment in Quarter Column.

CHAPTER II.

THE SURMA VALLEY LIGHT HORSE, 1886, TO THE MANIPUR CAMPAIGN.

IN August, 1886, the title of the Regiment was changed from the Cachar and Sylhet Mounted Rifles to the Surma Valley Light Horse. The old title was too unwieldy and did not stress the real unanimity that existed between the two halves of the Regiment, and with the change of title the Corps may be said to have passed out of its embryo stage. And though, at this date, it was very far from perfect, the Reports show how it gradually became more and more efficient and was recognised as one of the best Light Horse Regiments in India. In the list of the *Disposition of Volunteer Corps in Bengal under the Commander-in-Chief in India*, published in the Annual Report for 1885-86, the Surma Valley Light Horse is placed second to the Behar Light Horse, and is immediately followed by the Sibsagar Mounted Rifles. It is of interest to note that there were thirty-eight Volunteer Regiments in that list.

In 1887, Lieut.-Col. Knox-Wight resigned his command and was succeeded by Major A. Milne on the 20th May, who was promoted to Lieut.-Colonel. There is also a change of Adjutants, Captain G. F. Willes, 15th Bengal Cavalry, succeeding Lieut. Hatton.

The most important event of that year was that the Provincial Medal for the best shot amongst the Volunteers of the Province—Burma and Assam—was won by Captain Donald Ferguson.

There were two Camps of Exercise again this year; the Right Wing (Cachar) was inspected at Silchar on the 25th February and the Left Wing (Sylhet) at Kannyhatti on the 18th. The Inspecting Officer was Brig.-Gen. Sir F. B. Norman, and the Commander-in-Chief regards his report as "very satisfactory."

In 1888 the Surma Valley Light Horse begins to take its place among other military units. On the 2nd January the Corps paraded for the first time with the Brigade on the occasion of the proclamation of Queen Victoria as Empress of India, and towards the end of that year an escort was furnished for the Viceroy, the Marquis of Dufferin, when he visited Dacca. It was commanded by Captain M. J. Balfour, who was specially thanked and commended for the manner in which he handled the detachment, and the Commissioner of Dacca wrote to thank the men of the escort for their loyal assistance which had contributed to the success of the Viceroy's visit. His Excellency himself also expressed his appreciation and presented a photograph of himself to be hung up at the Regimental Headquarters, and also a medal to be competed for by members of the Corps, which curiously enough, was won by Captain Balfour in the following events :— Tent Pegging, Heads and Posts, Turk's Head and Lime Cutting, in which he scored 85 points out of a possible 100.

Sir Charles Elliot, Chief Commissioner of Assam, resigned in 1887. He had been Honorary Colonel and to mark his connection with the Surma Valley Light Horse he presented a cup (in 1888) to be shot for annually.

The Provincial Medal was won for the second time in succession—by Trooper B. A. Martin.

Sir F. B. Norman again inspected the Regiment and comments on the great improvements all round.

Although the Inspecting Officer's report is satisfactory, the Commandant is not by any means satisfied with the Regiment. In 1889 he writes in the Annual Report:—"I should not be doing my duty if I failed to call attention to the fact that there are a great number of non-efficients which ought to be impossible in a Corps like ours; and with so many proficient non-commissioned officers, and all combatant officers themselves proficients, troop officers ought to find no difficulty in arranging for a sufficient number of drills and target practices which each member could attend, and thus not only make himself efficient, but earn for the Corps the grant offered by Government. This money is urgently required to start a prize fund for the encouragement of shooting, so that prizes could be given, not necessarily only for the best shots, but that by a system of handicapping, or shooting in classes or troops, all might have an equal chance."

Two rifle matches were held that year. The Behar Light Horse beat the Right Wing by 387 points to 374, and the Darrang Mounted Rifles beat " C " Troop by 312 points to 306. Against this the Provincial Medal was won for the third time in succession for the Corps by Trooper E. J. Jones.

In 1890 the Camps of Exercise were a failure. There was a decrease in attendance and the Commandant is " unable to account for it satisfactorily." The Inspecting Officer again comments favourably on the Regiment, however, and Colonel Milne is congratulated on its efficiency. Three rifle matches were held that year, all of which were won. A picked team of the Corps shot against the Behar Light Horse and won by 420 points against 390. The Right Wing faced the same opponents and won by 378—340, and " E " Troop met the Calcutta Light Horse and won by the narrow margin of one point (384—383).

We are enabled to obtain a slight idea of the nature of the training from a newspaper account of that time. The Surma Valley was surrounded by Hill Tribes who were always liable to give trouble and the scattered nature of the country led to the training being more or less concentrated in troops. Skirmishing and attack in extended order formed the backbone of the work, and skeleton drill movements for the instruction of officers and non-commissioned officers were practised. A great deal of attention was paid to making the men proficient in the use of their rifles and other arms and this was encouraged by military sports. For this reason a number of competitions was instituted. The officers presented a challenge cup, which became known as the " Officers' Cup "; the funds of the Corps permitted a number of prizes being given for musketry; the Lloyd-Lindsay Competition had been introduced in the previous year, and other cups were presented for swordsmanship and shooting.

The Provincial Medal was won for the fourth year in succession by the corps and the second in succession by Trooper E. J. Jones.

In 1891 the Commandant regrets " to have to draw attention to the fact that the attendance at the Camp of Exercise was smaller than it has been during the last three years," yet at the same time the Inspecting Officer, Major-Gen. Collett, is full of praise for the Regiment and his report reflects great credit on Colonel Milne and all ranks under his command. He also added, little knowing that he was prophetic, that " The Surma Valley Light Horse will do good service if they ever get the chance." That chance came sooner than was expected. On the 23rd March, 1891, the Chief Commissioner of Assam, Mr. J. W. Quinton, and his Staff were murdered at Imphal, and a month later Manipur was occupied by British troops, the Surma Valley Light Horse forming part of the expedition—but that deserves a chapter to itself.

In the meantime the training fades under the glory of the Manipur Expedition. A shooting match was held between the Right Wing and the Behar Light Horse which was won by thirty points.

S. V. L. H. Karimganj Camp 1896
Officers' Sword Exercise.

CHAPTER III.

THE MANIPUR CAMPAIGN, 1891.

THE story of the Surma Valley Light Horse and the Manipur Expedition may first be told from the official orders and despatches. On the 9th April, 1891, Lieut.-Col. R. H. Rennick, Officer Commanding the Cachar Column, Manipur Field Force, issued the following order:—

CAMP CACHAR.
9th April, 1891.

A moving Post Office will accompany the Headquarters of the Column.

A Field Post Office will be opened at Jhiri Ghat.

Until such time as the Field Post Office is in working order, the Surma Valley Light Horse will carry all communications along the line Cachar-Barak."

On the 10th the following officer, non-commissioned officers and troopers were detailed to proceed at once to Jhiri Ghat:—

Captain A. J. M. MacLaughlin
Sergt-Major Kearney
Sergeant W. Townsend Smith
    „   H. Chamney
    „   Balkwill
Lce-Sergt. J. W. Sidey
Corporal W. Mason
Lce-Corporal F. W. Hight.

Trooper A. D. Forbes	Trooper J. G. Knowles
„ A. Ferrie	„ R. Ferris
„ P. Gordon	„ J. Grierson
„ A. W. Guise	„ G. Hunt Ross
„ H. Morris	„ A. Rose
„ T. L. Row	„ J. A. Sandeman
„ F. G. Steele	„ R. R. Evers

Trumpeter F. L. Brown-Constable

On the 15th April, Captain J. W. S. Dalrymple-Clark, Surma Valley Light Horse, was ordered to attach himself to the Staff of the Officer Commanding the Silchar Column as Honorary Orderly Officer.

* * * * *

Extract from Brigade Orders by Lieut.-Col. R. H. Rennick, Commanding the Silchar Column, Manipur Field Force.

CAMP GODAM GHAT.
6th May, 1891.

CASUALTIES.

It is with much regret that the Officer Commanding the Silchar Column has to announce the death of Trooper Ferris of the Surma Valley Light Horse, which took place on the night of the 30th April, of typhoid fever.

In doing so, the O. C. wishes to place on record his appreciation of the truly patriotic and gallant manner in which Trooper Ferris discharged his arduous and self-imposed duties, never sparing himself whenever there was a call made upon the Volunteers.

As an instance of his performance Trooper Ferris, who had already ridden thirty miles on the 17th April, did not hesitate to ride ten miles more to escort the Officer Commanding the Column from Lakhipur to Jhiri Ghat.

By Order,
(*Sd.*) ST. G. L. STEELE, CAPTAIN,
Brigade Major, Silchar Column,
Manipur Field Force.

* * * * *

29th June, 1891.

The following extract from the Proceedings of the Chief Commissioner of Assam, General Department, No. 335M, dated Shillong, 24th June, 1891 :—

Resolution on Services rendered by Colonel Milne and officers and men of the Surma Valley Light Horse, and the European Planters of the Cachar District.

Read the following letter from Major H. S. P. Maxwell, Chief Political Officer, Manipur, No. 47, dated 12th June, 1891 :—

"I have the honour to bring to the favourable notice of the Chief Commissioner, the great assistance I received from Colonel Milne, Commanding the Surma Valley Light Horse, the officers and men of the Regiment and the European gentlemen engaged in the tea industry in the Cachar District at the time when the news was first received of the outbreak in Manipur.

Several officers and men of the Surma Valley Light Horse took part later on in the march of the Silchar Column on Manipur, and their services have, I understand, been brought to the notice of the Government, and I would now place before the Chief Commissioner for special recognition of the Local Government the valuable assistance, as District Officer of Cachar, I received from Colonel Milne, Commanding the Surma Valley Light Horse, the officers and men of that Regiment and from the Tea Planters throughout the District."

RESOLUTION.

The Chief Commissioner desires most cordially to acknowledge the valuable assistance rendered by Colonel Milne, Commanding the Surma Valley Light Horse, as well as by the officers and men of that Regiment. Although the Regiment was not actually called upon to render active service, there can be no doubt, the Chief Commissioner thinks, that danger did exist at the time referred to of a rising among the Manipuris residing in the Cachar District. The danger was, however, considerably reduced by the fact that these people must have been fully aware that Colonel Milne's Regiment would be ready at the shortest notice to assist the local authorities and check their turbulent propensities.

* * * * *

1st August, 1891. The following extract from Lieut.-Col. R. H. F. Rennick's despatch, Commanding the Silchar Column, Manipur Field Force, as published in G. G. O. No. 585, dated Simla, 19th June 1891, is republished for information.

Dated Nongba,
The 23rd May, 1891.

In conclusion, I wish to place on record my appreciation of the splendid behaviour of both officers and men of the Silchar Column under the most trying circumstances. Exposed throughout the march to the inclemencies of the season, to hardship, sickness, and privation, all answered cheerfully to the call of duty, and worked with a zeal and energy rarely surpassed.

Where the conduct of all was admirable, it is difficult to single out any particular officers or men with a view to bringing forward their names for the favourable notice of His Excellency the Commander-in-Chief. I would, however, beg leave to mention specially the following in connection with the advance :—

CAPTAIN A. J. M. MACLAUGHLIN, *Commanding the Detachment of the Surma Valley Light Horse.*

* * * * *

That is the bald story from the official despatches and notices. In itself it is a brave record and reflects great credit and honour on a Corps then only eight years old. The Detachment was chiefly employed on the important duties of patrolling and carrying despatches. From the report of the Officer Commanding the Silchar Column it will be seen that they were labouring under conditions of great hardship. Moreover, every member of the

OFFICERS, 1897.

Surma Valley Light Horse Detachment had to provide his own horse and many of these were lost. One trooper, it is reported, not only had to bear the loss of his horse himself, but after he returned to his garden he received a bill from Government for forage supplied! Naturally he refused to pay and an attachment was served on his salary.

Two men died on active service—Troopers Ferris and Forbes, both of whom from enteric. Captain MacLaughlin was mentioned in despatches because he was selected to carry some important messages from Manipur to Silchar, and by dint of hard riding arrived at the Dilkhoosh Tea Estate in the record time of twenty-seven hours. When the Column reached Imphal the first man to enter the town was Sergeant H. Chamney who, with others of the Surma Valley Light Horse, did not wait for further developments in the infantry attack, but galloped straight in.

At first there was some difficulty about medals, for Government claimed that as the men were not " called out " they were not entitled to them, but eventually the services of the Detachment were recognised and the Indian Frontier Medal for the campaign was awarded.

There are few of those men left now, and I have been fortunate enough to persuade Captain (now Colonel) A. J. M. MacLaughlin to write his impressions of that time. They are therefore, given in his own words :—

"I have been trying to recall a little of what happened just before and during the Manipur Campaign, and shall now put it on record, giving in particular how a detachment of the Surma Valley Light Horse was accepted for service in Manipur. I have been told that this was the first time that a volunteer detachment was on active service, but for the correctness of this I cannot vouch.

"The first information I received of the trouble in Manipur was at Heroncherra (in Cachar) from a Manipuri carpenter, who brought the news that Grimwood had been killed on the previous day. It struck me as almost impossible for news to get down by a messenger over such a distance in so short a time, but this man assured me that such was possible with relays of ponies, as there were many short cuts through the hills. Moreover, at that time the moon was nearly full, so there was sufficient light for riding through the night.

"I immediately got into touch with Colonel Milne, who was then Commandant of the Surma Valley Light Horse, having found him on the Polo Ground at Barkhola, and suggested that I should mobilise "C" Troop, of which I was then Captain, and offer their services. Of this he approved and next morning, "C" Troop appeared before the Deputy Commissioner in Silchar ready for active service, except for rations and ammunition, which we expected to get in Silchar.

"The Deputy Commissioner was much astonished when he saw us and was told what I had heard. He said that so far as he knew nothing serious had occurred, but, he added, that there had been no news of the Chief Commissioner and his party for two days as telegraphic communication had been interrupted. He thanked us for offering our services so promptly and said he would be glad to accept them should they be needed.

"In about three weeks' time, the Chief Commissioner's escort under three British officers turned up in Silchar and with them was Mrs. Grimwood, but information was lacking as to the fate of the Chief Commissioner, Colonel Skeen, Mr. Grimwood, Cousins, etc., beyond that they had gone into the fort at Imphal and had not returned. It was reported that soon after the Chief Commissioner and his party had entered the fort, firing was opened—from rifles and two small guns from the outer walls of the fort—on the Residency and the escort, whereupon a retirement was ordered and a retreat to Silchar took place, instead of an assault which might possibly have saved the lives of the Chief Commissioner and his party.

"When it was arranged that a punitive force of three columns was to advance upon Imphal—one from Burma, one from Assam and one from Silchar—the services of a detachment of the Surma Valley Light Horse under me were accepted for service with the Silchar Column. An advance party of this column moved off from Silchar and took up a position on the Barak river on the far side of the Kalanugger ridge, and for over a week this detachment seemed to be unable to communicate with Silchar. The Surma Valley Light Horse was then ordered to get into touch with this detachment and this formed our first duty. On reaching the Kalanugger ridge a stockade was found, but the Manipuris who had been there disappeared on our arrival, and Sergeant Chamney, with some of the Volunteers, rode on to the Barak river where they found Colonel Brown and his detachment. A signal detachment was then sent to the top of the ridge—a distance of four or five miles—and communication by heliograph was opened up with Silchar.

" The detachment of the Surma Valley Light Horse then moved on in advance of Colonel Brown's infantry, keeping up communication with the frontier by patrols. The Manipuris kept retiring before us, but made it a point before doing so to burn the rest houses and other shelters before we arrived. This was very irritating, as we had, in consequence, to sleep on wet ground under rain nearly every night. One night we thought we were particularly lucky in finding some Naga houses that had not been burned, but from them we had to beat a hasty retreat during the night, having been driven out by fleas! Rain we could put up with—but not these.

" After this we decided to make our advances by night so as to reach each rest house and Manipuri camp by daybreak. This plan worked well, as the enemy, on getting the signal that we were upon them, made a hasty retreat and did not get time to burn the huts. By adopting these tactics we had comfortable sleeping accommodation for some nights.

" It may be wondered why the Manipuris were so frightened when they saw us coming. Well, I heard afterwards that they were told by the Nagas that all the Cachar and Sylhet planters were coming on horseback to hunt down and kill any Manipuris they could find, to avenge the death of Cousins, who had been very popular with them while acting as Sub-divisional Officer at Karimganj. This dread of us was shown very clearly on one occasion. Half-way between Bishanpore and Imphal I was reconnoitring with a few men, and I was a little in advance when I came on about two hundred Manipuris behind earthworks. I need not mention how quickly I retreated, but not any faster than they, for they fled without even troubling to fire at me! I thought they would not stop running until they had reached Imphal. But not so; because the next day they were there to try and oppose the advance of our infantry, and retired only a short distance on to the neighbouring hills from which they opened fire, but without inflicting any casualties.

"While bivouacking for a night, about six miles or so from Imphal, numerous fires were observed at that place, and when we reached it the next day we found that any buildings that might have provided shelter for us were burned down, except a large iron-roofed theatre and a few small lines close to it. In the cellars underneath the theatre a large quantity of gunpowder was found—which was used later to blow up the Sacred Dragons, close to which, it came to be known, all those who ventured into the fort with a view to a peaceful settlement were executed. In the small lines there were also many baskets of dynamite; I saw a powder trail leading towards the iron-roofed theatre by which it was probably intended to explode the powder under the theatre. This had failed as it had got wet from an extraordinarily heavy shower of rain which fell as our column entered the fort. It was seen fizzling and put out."

* * * * *

This chapter may well be concluded with the final remarks made by the Commander-in-Chief in his letter of the 5th August, 1891. "It is to be noted that the General Officer Commanding

Assam District states that 'The Surma Valley Light Horse will do good service if ever they get the chance,' and Major-General Collett's remarks have been fully verified by the excellent work performed by members of the Corps with the Silchar Column during the late Manipur operations."

CHAPTER IV.

From 1892 to the South African War.

THE Manipur Campaign seems to have taken all the energy out of the Surma Valley Light Horse. The Commandant complains that "the attendance at the annual inspection—1892—with the exception of "C" and "D" Troops, was most disappointing, and it is not creditable to the Corps as a whole that this should be so. Many more members could doubtless have turned up had they made any real effort to do so. I hope our next meet will tell a very different story, for none of us ought to rest content until the Surma Valley Light Horse can do what other Corps, composed somewhat similarly, have succeeded in doing; and that is, to parade once a year as a Regiment and be inspected as such, with an attendance of at least half the members present. There are difficulties to be met, no doubt, owing to the peculiar composition and location of the Corps—such as long distances, defective means of travelling, great expense, difficulty in being absent from gardens for any length of time; but all these difficulties can be surmounted by mutual support and a resolve on the part of the members to do what they can to bring about the good end. An opportunity will be afforded you of meeting all in one spot and parading as a Regiment during the course of the present season, and I earnestly hope this new departure will commend itself to you all and turn out a great success. It would no doubt be far more satisfactory to the Government to have the Corps inspected as a whole, rather than at two or three different centres, while officers and men alike would profit more from their week's instruction."

For the first year since the Corps competed the Provincial Medal was not won, and the only thing that relieves the drabness of 1892 was that Colonel Milne was appointed Honorary Aide-de-Camp to His Excellency the Commander-in-Chief, Sir Frederick Sleigh Roberts, v.c.

There was a change of Adjutants during that year, Captain H. M. Johnston, 15th Bengal Lancers, succeeding to that office.

The Commandant writes in a much more hopeful tone in 1893. "At last the reproach has been taken away from us that this Corps alone, amongst the bigger Mounted Corps in India, was unable to muster a hundred men for the annual inspection. That can no longer be said, and I hope it will never again be said about us with truth. The difficulties of travelling remained as before but, thanks to a determined effort on the part of officers and men, these difficulties were alike surmounted, and for the first time in our history we were able to meet in respectable numbers, and be inspected as a Regiment. The site chosen for our meeting was Karimganj, which is fairly central and convenient for the whole Corps, and will probably remain such until our railway is running, when many of the present difficulties will disappear. Our meet was a great success both professionally and socially and I trust that future ones will be even more so. To the men joining it, as well as to the Government, such a muster is far more profitable and satisfactory than those we have held in former years, so every one should do his best to be present next time if possible."

In the Birthday Honours list of that year a Companionship of the Indian Empire was conferred on Colonel Milne, the first decoration awarded to an officer in the Regiment, if we except the "mention in despatches" of Captain MacLaughlin. Colonel Milne had thoroughly earned his decoration. He had been connected with the Corps from its commencement and during the whole time had been its mainstay. In his report for 1893-94 he traces the history of the Regiment since he assumed command and comments on its gradual advance towards perfection. One point is worthy of notice, the Surma Valley Light Horse had won the Provincial Medal six times out of eight years. This year it had been won by Trooper D. W. Elder. A Carbine Club, which had been started in the previous year, was closed down, partly because of the meagre support given to it, and partly because the Assam Rifle Association had been started.

The year 1894 shows a general all-round improvement. Shooting is better and there is a marked advance both in appearance and drill at the annual inspection. Trooper A. Rose won the Provincial Medal. Apart from this there is little of interest to note in that year, except that at a shooting match held in October for members of Volunteer Corps in the Assam District, the second and third places are secured by members of the Surma Valley Light Horse—Trooper J. T. Mawhood and Sergeant R. T. Fraser.

Colonel Milne resigned his command on the 1st March, 1895, and was succeeded by Lieut.-Col. Eden Showers on the 29th March.

The strength of the Regiment was now 326 against 284 of the previous year. The attendance at Camp was good, one hundred and forty-nine members attending. " The turn-out of the Regiment was very satisfactory, the horses were of a useful stamp and looked serviceable, the bridles were all of the regimental pattern and there was more uniformity about the saddles . . . . . . In conclusion, I congratulate the Corps on its efficiency and smart appearance, and thank all ranks for the support they have rendered me. I would remind them, however, that we have not yet reached the standard to be aimed at, and continued exertions on the part of all are necessary before we can with sincerity whisper even to ourselves that we are " ' Second to None,' " writes Colonel Showers.

The General Officer's Cup, open to all Volunteers in Assam, and presented by Major-Gen. R. M. Jennings, c. b., was won by Sergeant J. Purves.

1896 seems to be a very dull year. The Commandant reports that though the strength of the Corps shows a decrease, the general efficiency undoubtedly shows an increase. The Rifle match for the G. O. C.'s Cup was won by Trooper A. Rose with Lce.-Sergt. D. Taylor as runner up.

Towards the end of 1896 a Rifle Match was held between "C" Troop and the Shillong Volunteer Rifles which was won by 474 points to 457.

The Camp of Exercise in 1897 took a novel form. Instead of being confined to the Surma Valley Light Horse alone, it was attended by the Assam Mounted Guns, a Detachment of the 17th Bengal Infantry, and a Detachment of the Surma Valley Military Police Battalion, the whole camp being under the command of the General Officer Commanding, Assam District. The work done was certainly more instructive than at any other camp. Field firing at night by the light of star shells from the Mountain Battery, field operations with a combined attack of infantry and cavalry under cover of the guns, and throwing a bridge across the Longai river formed part of the training. The Surma Valley Light Horse covered itself with credit, both in the work done and in the numbers attending, which with one hundred and fifty-eight provided a record.

The Provincial Medal was again won by Trooper A. Rose, but a shooting match between the Regiment and the 17th Bengal Infantry was not so successful. In the revolver section the latter Regiment won by 130 points to 88, and the rifle event was also won by the Bengal Infantry with a score of 421 points against 400.

During this year Captain Johnston, the Adjutant, retired, and for a few months Lieut. T. E. Madden of the 17th Bengal Infantry undertook the duties, and on 16th April, Lieut. A. C. H. Smithett, 15th Bengal Lancers, was appointed.

The site of the Camp was changed from Karimganj to Lungla in 1898, and the result was a slight falling off in attendance. Rumours went round that the Camp must be a failure, that there was no water, no grass obtainable for the horses, and that the site selected was a hot-bed of cholera, but, as usual, everything went as smoothly as in previous years. The Commandant explains the reason for the change of site.

"1. Karimganj had been the site for four years, the country round was well known, and there is no new ground for manœuvres.

2. The nearer we are to Calcutta the more chance there is of the Commander-in-Chief, the Lieutenant-General

Commanding, or the Inspector-General of Cavalry coming to inspect us.

3. As Volunteers our duty is to protect the District. I do not for a moment suppose that there is any occasion for alarm, yet, should there be discontent, the fact that one hundred and fifty mounted men, armed and ready for service, can be assembled in a few days must have a powerful effect on the native community, and for this reason the more we move our camps about the better.

After this explanation, and the proof from the last camp that fresh sites do not mean failure, I trust there will be no shirking from the next camp."

The Provincial Medal was won by Corporal T. H. Knolles, but 1898 is not so good as other years. For one reason there was a very bad tea season and reductions in the European establishment on many gardens were considered necessary, with the result that forty-eight men left the Surma Valley. Towards the end of that year—on the 26th of August—sanction was granted for the formation of a new troop, to be designated "G" Troop, and its headquarters were in the Luskerpore Valley.

The Camp of Exercise of 1899 was held in December and was the best attended since combined camps were instituted. It was inspected by Lieut.-Gen. Sir George Luck, K. C. B., Commanding in Bengal. During that year Sergeant T. S. Mulligan won the Provincial Medal and a Carbine Competition between the Regiment and the Calcutta Light Horse resulted in a win for the former by 191 points to 152.

On the 1st January, 1900, Colonel Showers resigned his command and was succeeded by Lieut.-Col. A. J. M. MacLaughlin. On the 1st February, Colonel Showers was appointed to be Second-in-Command, with the rank of Major, of the Indian Mounted Cavalry Corps (Lumsden's Horse), which was then in process of formation for the war in South Africa, and three other officers from the Corps were accepted for service:—Henry

"B" Company Lumsden's Horse.
Surma Valley Light Horse Contingent.
South African War 1900.

Chamney, Charles Lyon Sidey, and Dr. Samuel Arthur Powell. In addition to these, the following members of the Surma Valley Light Horse were accepted for active service:—

G. E. P. Thesiger, A. E. Chartres, W. Townsend Smith, J. Maclaine, A. P. Woodright, E. B. Moir-Byres, R. G. Hunter-Musket, W. E. C. Johnson, J. A. Burn-Murdock, B. S. Chapman, S. Ducat, C. A. Forbes, O. S. Hamilton, A. W. Harrison, R. J. Innes, R. B. Lungley, M. H. Logan, A. Lytle, P. J. Partridge, W. Reid, J. W. Stevenson, J. Sinclair, B. C. A. Stuart, C. W. Spicer, W. Turnbull, E. A. Thelwall, and W. R. Winder.

The services of the Surma Valley Light Horse in South Africa will be recorded in the next chapter, and it will be sufficient to mention here that the death in action of Colonel Showers was regretted by the whole Regiment, as also was the death from disease of Serg.-Farrier J. Maclaine.

Major H. Chamney received a Companionship of the Order of St. Michael and St. George, and Captain Sidey and Surgeon-Captain S. A. Powell were mentioned in despatches for having "rendered special and meritorious service."

CHAPTER V.

THE SOUTH AFRICAN WAR.

ON the 9th January, 1900, the news was made public that the offer of Lieut.-Col. D. M. Lumsden, formerly of the Assam Valley Light Horse, to raise a body of Mounted Volunteers for service in South Africa, had been accepted. Colonel Lumsden's original proposal was to raise a force of two hundred mounted infantry and, towards their equipment, he offered a handsome donation of half a lakh of rupees. His Excellency the Viceroy, in consultation with the Commander-in-Chief in India, telegraphed the offer to the Secretary of State who laid it before the War Office, with the result that it was accepted and Colonel Lumsden was appointed Commandant of the Corps he proposed to raise.

As might have been expected, the Corps was strongly supported from Assam, the Surma Valley and Behar. In the first two districts Colonel Lumsden was very well known and he had all the volunteers at his back. He immediately became the "man of the hour" in Assam and the Surma Valley, and enthusiasm mounted to white heat. Cachar and Sylhet set a subscription on foot to supply the outfit of those who had been selected from the Surma Valley, and money came in at a great rate.

On the 12th January, Colonel Lumsden arrived in Calcutta from Australia, and immediately commenced the work of organisation. For many weeks he was probably the busiest man in India, for offers poured in to him from all sides and he had to make his selection. Two companies of Volunteers were raised consisting in all of 251 men and 265 horses.

On 9th February the camp, which had originally been pitched near the Zeerut Bridge, was moved to the Maidan, south of Fort William. The contingents of the Surma Valley Light Horse and Assam Valley Light Horse were the first to arrive and the Behar Light Horse joined just before the site of the camp was

"B" Company Lumsden's Horse.
Departure from Calcutta for South African War 1900.

changed, and on the 10th February Lumsden's Horse was in full muster.

On the afternoon of the 14th there was a farewell service at St. Paul's Cathedral at which the Lord Bishop of Calcutta gave an address, during which he said—"The men of Lumsden's Horse are going to South Africa with a deep solemnity of purpose, as men who have undertaken a task from which they might, without reproach, have held aloof, and a sure conviction that they are playing a part not unworthy of the British race and the British Empire."

"B" Company, in which was the Detachment of the Surma Valley Light Horse, sailed on the 3rd of March by the "Ujina," and arrived at Durban on the 24th, where they got their first news of the war since they left India, and heard that Lord Roberts had occupied Bloemfontein and that the "Lindula" with "A" Company had proceeded to Cape Town three days before. They disembarked at East London on the 26th, with orders to proceed to Bloemfontein, and on the 28th entrained for Bethulie, but detrained the next day at Queenstown where they stayed until April 4th, as the wagons were needed elsewhere. On the 4th a march was begun to Bethulie, but on the 6th they found trucks waiting for them at Stockbron, into which they got, forty to fifty men per truck.

Eventually they reached Bethulie on the 7th and there received orders to detrain once more. This was completed by 2 a.m. and at 4-30 a.m. they were ordered to saddle up and be ready to march as an escort for six hundred mules to Bloemfontein. Their next halting place was Spiersfontein, nineteen miles distant, which they left again on the 9th and arrived at Springfontein at 3 p.m. where they were informed that they were to start again next morning as escort to a Maxim Gun Battery, which was proceeding to Bloemfontein, in addition to the mules.

The Special Correspondent of the *Indian Daily News*, writes of this time :—" I may mention that one section of our Company always acted as advance guard, and the advance guard again threw out scouts in front and on the flanks; the duty of the scouts being to search the kopjes on either side of the road and communicate with the main body by hand signals, should any enemy appear in sight."

The Corps left Springfontein on the morning of the 10th and marched sixteen miles to Jaggersfontein; and the following morning they set off intending to do fifteen miles, but owing to the heavy rain the camping ground was under water and they pushed on another eight miles until they reached Edenburg. There they found the ground inches deep in water and they had no tents. So, wrapping themselves up in their blankets, they slept where and how they could.

On the 12th they were on the move again and camped at Bethany. Here a night attack was expected and the men of the Maxim Gun Battery "stood to" all night on an adjacent hill, while thirty men of the Corps accompanied them as an extra protection. The next day—the 13th—they resumed their march and arrived at Kaffir River in the afternoon. The following morning they received their first "Home Mail," one of the men of "A" Company, then at Bloemfontein, having been sent down with it. That afternoon they marched to Karlspruit and into Bloemfontein the following day, having marched one hundred and sixty miles.

Sir Arthur Conan Doyle, in *The Great Boer War* (page 369), gives an interesting description of the troops in Bloemfontein. " The streets of the little Dutch town formed, during this interval, a curious object lesson in the resources of the Empire. All the scattered Anglo-Celtic races had sent their best blood to fight for the common cause . . . . . . To stand in the market square of Bloemfontein and to see the warrior types around you was to be assured of the future of the race. The middle-sized, square-set, weather-tanned, straw-bearded British Regulars crowded the footpaths. There might one see the hard-faced Canadians, the loose-limbed dashing Australians—fire-blooded and keen—the dark New Zealanders, with a Maori touch here and there in their features, the

Lieut.-Col. E. C. Showers.
1895-1899

gallant men of Tasmania, the gentlemen troopers of India and Ceylon, and everywhere the wild South African Irregulars."

On the 21st they left Bloemfontein, halting at Glen *en route*, arriving at Spytfontein on the 22nd. The units in the Corps to which they were attached were:—

        Lumsden's Horse
        Loch's Horse (a detachment)
        West Riding and Oxford
        8th Regiment of Mounted Infantry.

These, in all about 740 strong, were under the command of Colonel Ross, to whom they reported at Spytfontein. That evening they received orders to start at 4-30 a.m. for Kranz Krall, which was done in company with the 14th Brigade, their object being to prospect a bridge about eight miles on the main road to Bloemfontein which the Boers intended to destroy. They were only just in time to prevent them carrying out their object, and the night was spent at the bridge, returning to Spytfontein next day. Nothing eventful occurred during the next few days, but on the 30th Lumsden's Horse received its baptism of fire, though a detachment of that Corps, operating ten miles east of Karee Siding above Glen, repulsed a party of Boers on the 27th.

On the evening of the 29th Colonel Ross received orders that the Corps was to make a demonstration next morning at daybreak on the right flank of the Boer lines for the purpose of drawing them from their position and enabling the 14th Brigade under General Maxwell, which was to have come up on their right, to get behind and cut them off.

The Mounted Infantry portion of General Tucker's force joined hands with Colonel Ross's Corps half a mile from the camp. A portion of the Corps was ordered to occupy Gun Kopje about four miles on the left. Colonel Lumsden, with Major Showers, Captains Rutherford, Clifford and Chamney, Lieuts. Sidey and Pugh, went forward with the right flank.

The next section is taken from a report written by Colonel Lumsden on 17th May 1900. "Shortly after arrival, the Boers took up a position on a kopje about 1,500 yards directly in front, and soon opened rifle fire on our position. Fortunately our men had time to ensconce themselves behind rocks, and consequently, though bullets were falling freely, were able to maintain a steady fire on the enemy without exposing themselves. It was here I deeply regret to say that Major Showers met his death. He was on the extreme right of the firing line and exposed to the flanking fire of the Boers who had moved a party into a *donga* some 300 or 400 yards to their left. I personally begged him not to expose himself, as also did Captains Chamney and Rutherford, but he would stand erect using his field-glasses and presenting a most conspicuous mark for the enemy's fire, which resulted fatally to him shortly after noon, a Mauser bullet entering his right side half-way down and coming out through his left arm above the elbow . . . . . . there was a heavy fire on the spot where he fell and it was with much danger and difficulty that Captain Powell and Captain Chamney and others succeeded in removing him from the summit of the hill to a place of safety about 30 yards down. Early in the morning I ordered Private Chartres with eight men to occupy a kopje 800 yards to our right to prevent the Boers turning our right, and which he held until ordered to retire. It was a small party for this important position, but under the circumstances no more could be spared, I having only about 60 men with me, 20 of whom under Lieut. Sidey were detached by Colonel Ross to protect the Vicker's Maxim (commonly styled "Pompoms") in the centre of the position."

The *Indian Daily News* of the 3rd May, 1900, refers to this battle :—"We now learn from *Reuter* that Lumsden's Horse have not only been in action during the recent operations near Thaba N'chu, but they have suffered heavily, as among the killed is an officer of whom we in Bengal were particularly proud. Major Showers, the gallant second in command, who left India in charge of "B" Company, has been killed, and his death will cause the utmost regret in Assam, where, when he commanded the Surma Valley Light Horse, he was recognised as the smartest Volunteer officer in the District and one of the ablest in the whole of India. It seems only the other day that he laid down the command of the Surma Valley Light Horse, after bringing that Corps to a state of perfection equal to that of any crack regiment of Regulars. Major Showers was among the first of Colonel Lumsden's volunteers, and it did not affect his enthusiasm in the least that he had to serve under his old subordinate . . . . . . Among the wounded we are sorry to find the name of Private J. H. Burn-Murdoch . . . . . . Lumsden's Horse have been blooded, and the whole of India will be proud that our volunteers have behaved with the credit thatwas expected of them.'

A further incident in this battle is given in *The Great Boer War* (page 399). "Having got to the north of the British forces, Botha made no effort to get away, but turned at bay on the first good position he could find. This was at Houtnek, to the northwest of Thab N'chu. Out of this he was driven in a two days' action by Hamilton . . . . . . After this victory, Hamilton's men, who had fought for seven days out of ten, halted for a rest at Jacobsrust . . . . . . Before entering on a description of this great and decisive movement for the central advance, one small action calls for comment. This was the cutting off of twenty men of Lumsden's Horse in a reconnaissance at Karee. The small post under Lieut. Crane found themselves by some misunderstanding isolated in the midst of the enemy. Refusing to hoist the flag of shame they fought their way out, losing half their number, while of the other half, it is said, that there was not one who could not show bullet marks upon his clothes or person. The men of this Corps, Volunteer Anglo-Indians, had abandoned the ease and even luxury of Eastern life for the hard fare and rough fighting of this most trying campaign. In coming they had set the whole Empire an object lesson in spirit, and now on their first field they set the army an example of military virtue. The proud traditions of Outram's Volunteers have been upheld by the men of Lumsden's Horse."

On 5th May, the London *Daily Graphic* published a report "from the Boer side":—"General Foroneman and General P. de Wet were engaged with the British in the vicinity of Thaba N'chu on Sunday. To-day the British came out about ten miles from Brandfort . . . . . and about 500 Federals drove them back as far as their entrenchment. The Federals found four dead on the field and took seventeen prisoners, most of whom were slightly hurt or wounded. Among the prisoners is Lieut. Crane of Lumsden's Horse. He informed me that this was his first engagement. When I told him that prisoners had been taken from other companies besides his own, the young officer said, "Well, I suppose that's some consolation'."

Colonel Lumsden's narrative may be resumed here:—" I cannot speak too highly of the gallant behaviour of my officers and men throughout the day. Individual instances of heroism were numerous and I much fear that, especially in Lieutenant Crane's section, many of the casualties were caused by men endeavouring to assist their wounded comrades. Mr. Crane himself was wounded in the groin, and I understand that Private Daubeney's and Private Case's deaths were due to their declining to leave their wounded officer as, judging from the number of empty cartridge cases found beside them, they must have kept up a fire on the advancing Boers to the last . . . . . . The same evening about four, Dr. Powell with the ambulance *tonga* and Private Godden proceeded under the red cross flag to search for the wounded, but in the gathering darkness was only able to reach the body of Major Showers who died previous to our retirement . . . . . Captain Powell, in endeavouring to return to Camp, lost his way and had to remain during the night on the veldt, reaching camp soon after daylight next morning. Soon after his arrival he returned with another search party, but found the Boers had already buried

FUNERAL OF COLONEL SHOWERS IN SOUTH AFRICA.
1900

THE SALUTE TO COLONEL SHOWERS
SOUTH AFRICA 1900.

the bodies of Privates Case, Daubeney, and Lumsden after having read the burial service over them. The remains of Major Showers, being found still unburied, were brought back and interred with military honours at the foot of the kopje behind our camp . . . . . . Subsequent to our return to Camp I was much gratified to receive from Colonel Ross, the Corps Commander, and Colonel Henry, the Brigade Commander, congratulations on the behaviour of my officers and men throughout the day, and on the following morning General Tucker, the Divisional Commander, came over in person for the same purpose, but at the same time read me a lecture on the inadvisability of allowing my men to attempt to bring off their wounded comrades when under fire, pointing out that it only drew fire on the wounded men and endangered their own lives for no adequate result, as the Boers were a very humane foe and treated the wounded carefully; that their first duty was to their Queen and Country and as soldiers they must remember such. The Boers subsequent to the fight were most courteous in their attentions and returned papers, rings, watches, money, etc. found on the bodies."

On the 3rd May, the Corps left Spytfontein and swept the country towards Brantfort. A little desultory fighting occurred, and the enemy's advance parties were driven in on to their positions. On the 4th the Crops halted, " with no food for the horses and only biscuits for the men," says Colonel Lumsden. On the 5th they were on the march again, most of it being done on foot to ease the tired horses, and in the afternoon they were told to head for De Vet Railway Station which the Boers held in force. They crossed the De Vet River just before dark and turned the Boer right under a heavy shell fire.

The 6th and 7th saw them scouring the country and still marching steadily, and on the 8th they did flank guard for the infantry during a march of twenty miles. On the 9th they were in action again. The Zand River found the enemy in considerable strength and they were expected to put up a great deal of opposition.

Our Corps here got the first definite order we had had yet and that was 'to keep in touch with the enemy at any cost,' and as this came from Lord Roberts direct we proceeded to obey it to the letter, with the result that we were under shell and rifle fire for the remainder of the day." *

The river was crossed and the march on Kronstadt began on the 10th. An early start was made on the 11th for the expected big fight at Kronstadt, for it was reported that the Boers were strongly posted five miles in front of the town. After a cautious advance for ten miles it was discovered that the position had been vacated, leaving Kronstadt undefended. Lord Roberts reported that "the procession entering the town was headed by my bodyguard, all of them Colonials." Here they waited for supplies before advancing on Pretoria.

"The rest has been a welcome one, as our horses are fairly done and I doubt if I could mount 150 men to-morrow, and a few more weeks' work like that of the last would reduce the number to 100 . . . . . . You can form no idea of the condition of our horses and had it not been that we have been able to commandeer and get remounts *en route* we should have half the Corps dismounted. We have lost quite 75 horses already and have stated officially that we require 75 remounts more and these we expect to get this afternoon. Mr. Barrow's *Molly Riley* looks like a bathing-machine horse . . . . . . The men are all very well and in good spirits, are most efficient cooks, and if allowed would rank high as looters, but orders against this are very strict and our men pay liberally for anything in the shape of foodstuffs when procurable."*

"The Corps halted at Kronstadt until the 22nd and on that day they moved out four and a half miles to a fresh camp. The next three days were spent in long weary marches, reconnoitring the country in front of the main advance, for they had been transferred at Kronstadt from General Hamilton's Column to the troops selected to march with Lord Roberts. Nothing was seen

---
*Colonel Lumsden's Report. *Vide Supra.*

LIEUT.-COL. A. J. M. MACLAUGHLIN, C.I.E.
1900-1907

of the enemy until the 26th when he was met at the Vaal River. A general advance of the 8th Corps was made dismounted and the Boers were driven back, " much to the delight of the Manager of the mines, who had been in a state of great anxiety. He treated all officers to breakfast and told us that the Boers had not expected us to arrive for two days, and that on the very morning the party we had just turned out had arrived with the intention of blowing up his mines . . . . . . He estimated that one million sterling has been saved." *

"On the 27th, the horses were turned out to graze and the men had received permission to go into the town and general clearing-up began, when suddenly at 10-30 a.m. they were ordered to move at once to help the 3rd Cavalry Brigade under General Gordon who was reported to be in a tight position to the northeast. Horses were caught and the corps was away by eleven o'clock, with no rations for man or horse. They proceeded with caution through a difficult piece of country, and arrived at the place where General Gordon was supposed to be at 4-30 p.m. But there were no signs of him, and they struggled on until the horses began to give out and the whole brigade encamped at 8 p.m. At 4-30 a.m. the following morning they were away again, but no Boers were seen and the Klip River was crossed without a shot being fired.

"On the 28th, we marched at 5-30, expecting to arrive after 10 miles at Natal Spruit, where fighting was certain. Our maps and information were, however, wrong for we found ourselves most unexpectedly in sight of the place with the smoke of the train leaving the station. We were sent to endeavour to cut if off as it would go through the kopjes and had a very exciting gallop of three miles, blowing up the railway behind the train. Again we pushed on to try and cut her off at the next big bend but again were too late, running into the fire of the party covering the retreat of the train. We then took up a position covering the railroad, while under Colonel Ross' orders a party

---
*Colonel Lumsden's Report.

of five men were sent to block the line at any cost. This very dangerous task was given to Lieutenant Pugh and the undermentioned men, who carried it through with great determination and coolness:—Privates Turner, Were, Dagge and Parks."*

From now on until the 1st June the Corps marched on, with desultory fighting, towards Johannesburgh, and on that day they arrived in time to see the Union Jack hoisted over the Fort which was entered unopposed. On the morning of the 3rd they marched twelve miles towards Pretoria, meeting with no resistance. On the 4th they advanced on Six Mile Spruit, being the leading regiment of the advanced brigade, expecting a fight as the Spruit was said to be the last position of the Boers and was to be desperately contested. But it was discovered that the Spruit was not held, and again they advanced and came into touch with the enemy at midday, who opened up with shell fire. The Boers were securely entrenched and it was difficult to dislodge them, but at 4 p.m. the firing slackened and eventually ceased and the position was evacuated.

"The 5th June was the day on which we reached the goal we had been struggling for. Pretoria at last! Not fighting our way in as anticipated by everybody, but a peaceful procession in with our baggage behind us, news having arrived that the Governor had surrendered the town late the previous night. We were not allowed to halt, just passing through the city and out to Irene, a station ten miles south of Pretoria and on the Johannesburgh line, which we at present occupy, the whole Corps protecting the rail from Pretoria to Johannesburgh :—"A" Company Headquarters taking the first ten miles, "B" Company the second and the remainder of the 8th Corps in detachments all down the line. We are here indefinitely awaiting events"†.

Except for a few small actions the work of Lumsden's Horse was practically completed. As Colonel Lumsden says in his letter dated 5th June—"It is considered that the war is virtually over and I fancy within a short time all Volunteer Corps

---

* Colonel Lumsden's Report.
† Colonel Lumsden's Report.

FORDING A RIVER
S. V. L. H. IN SOUTH AFRICA 1900.

BOERS, 1900

will be disbanded!" In that letter he gives a general description of what had happened—" . . . . . . I can only put 90 mounted men, including officers, into the field. This, considering the Corps landed with a full complement of 250 horses, and has since received nearly 150 remounts, will give you an idea of what we have gone through and the wear and tear our horses have had through marching and short feeding. Taking it as a whole, officers and men have kept excellent health, the only prevalent disease being dysentery. Our casualties have amounted to 25, just ten per cent. of the force we landed with; but this percentage must be nearly doubled considering that the most we ever put into the field was 186 and we are now reduced to under 100 mounted men.

"We have heard of the release of our prisoners and expect them to join us in a few days. Our only casualties in this shape were those taken on the 30th April at Flakfontein. I cannot say too much in praise of the conduct of my officers and men from first to last, under many hardships and under very trying circumstances, and I feel sure they have gained a name for themselves which their many friends, both in England and India, have just cause to be proud of."

On 22nd November, the first two parties left Pretoria by train for Cape Town on their way home. The press in England joined in a peon of praise for the gallant work done by the Corps, of which the following are extracts :—

The Daily Telegraph under the heading "Lumsden's Heroes" writes :—

The Regiment holds an excellent record and the behaviour of the men has been throughout admirable. Their casualties were :—At Spytfontein, eighteen; at Brandfort, one; at Zand River, two; at the Vaal, one; and at Pretoria, one. In subsequent operations they were highly commended. The Regiment was raised in Calcutta on 17th February last and left there early in March. It had an enthusiastic send-off, the members being entertained by the Viceroy of India, the Lieutenant-Governor, and the Metropolitan of Calcutta. The Indian public subscribed £30,000 for its formation and Colonel Lumsden himself gave £3,500. Major Showers, who was second in command, was killed at Spytfontein. The Corps comprises representatives of Behar, Surma Valley, Assam, Sylhet, Cachar, Mysore, Coorg Oudh, Cawnpore, the Punjab, and every part of India. It is essentially composed of gentlemen, who, on enlisting, were required to show that they were expert riders and shots, and could provide trained chargers. Of 1,500 applicants only 268 were selected.

Lumsden's Horse have been thanked twice in despatches and personally by Lord Roberts, Generals French, Mahon, Tucker, and Dickson, and Colonels Ross and Hickman. Many of the men have accepted civil employment in South Africa, twenty have been granted commissions in the Army, one entered the Navy, and three have joined the Police. The Regiment's best work was done in the van of Lord Roberts' march to Pretoria.

The Daily Mail:—Lumsden's Horse left to-day on their return to India. Their record throughout the campaign has been admirable and their total casualties are ten per cent. of their number.

The *Daily Graphic* and the *Pall Mall Gazette*, among other newspapers, contain references in similar strain.

*   *   *   *

Throughout this chapter in the history of the Surma Valley Light Horse it has been difficult to distinguish the particular work of the Regiment from the general work of Lumsden's Horse. Possibly this is the correct way to estimate the case, for the glory that came to Lumsden's Horse also come to " B " Company of that Corps—the Surma Valley Light Horse.

"Goodbye Brother Boer" South Africa, 1900

Leaving Cape Town. Homeward Bound, 1900

Surma Valley Light Horse Leaving South Africa, 1900

CHAPTER VI.

1901—1914

WRITING on 1st June, 1901, the Commandant (Lieut.-Col. A. J. M. MacLaughlin) says that the general situation shows a great improvement on the previous year. The strength of the Corps was 319, an increase of two, although many members had left the District or remained in South Africa. Fourteen members of the Surma Valley Light Horse Detachment with Lumsden's Horse had returned to the Corps, and "I must take this opportunity of welcoming them back and thanking them for the splendid way in which they have helped with their other comrades in upholding the honor of the S. V. L. H., under conditions which must have tried the endurance and pluck of many men . . . . . . The Corps has been honoured also by the presentation of five commissions in His Majesty's army, three of which have been accepted, and others of the Corps remain in South Africa in positions of trust under the existing Government there. It is also with very great pleasure I announce the fact that Major H. Chamney has been gazetted a Companion of the Order of St. Michael and St. George for his services as second in command of Lumsden's Horse."

During this year Queen Victoria died (23rd January) and His Majesty King Edward VII was proclaimed King of Great Britain and Ireland and Emperor of India, on 24th January.

The "Sirocco Cup," presented by Messrs. Davidson and Co., Belfast, for a shooting competition between Officers and men of the Surma Valley Light Horse, Assam Valley Light Horse and the Northern Bengal Mounted Rifles, was won by a member of this Regiment for the first time, the winner being Lieut. A. H. A. Meredith, and two Inter-Regimental Shooting Matches, between the Corps and the 5th Bengal Light Infantry, were contested. The first was won by the Surma Valley Light Horse by 373 points to 369, and the second by the 5th Bengal Light Infantry with a score of 616 points against 586.

The year 1902 reports further improvement, though the numbers have decreased to 308, men remaining in South Africa being the cause. " A great feature of the drill this year has been the introduction of shooting from horseback. Nearly all the horses now in the Corps will stand this, and with a little training and proper handling will stand steady; but it is useless to train them for this purpose, unless good shooting is made by their riders," writes the Commandant.

The Regiment was inspected by the Inspector-General of Volunteers in India (Major-General W. Hill) and also by Brigadier-General C. R. MacGregor, the General Officer Commanding the District. " The Inspecting Officers were good enough to praise the Corps in certain branches of their work, but we must not suppose therefore that we cannot improve."

Major-General Hill's own report reads as follows :—

" The general efficiency of this Corps is very satisfactory and creditable to all ranks. It appeared to me that almost every resident in the Surma Valley identifies himself with the Light Horse; those who cannot join as Troopers become Honorary Members and assist with their subscriptions.

" The *esprit-de-corps* that permeates all ranks seems to have spread throughout the Valley, and the ladies (a large number of whom were at Cachar during the Camp) appeared to be as keen and enthusiastic about the efficiency of the Corps as the men themselves. . . . . .

" The work done during the Camp at Cachar was practical and there was plenty of it. The dismounted work was very good and the scouting and reconnoitring as satisfactory as could be expected, considering the very few opportunities they have for studying a science that requires much study and the most careful and constant practice."

In the year under notice, the Assam Provincial Medal was won by Lieut. A. H. A. Meredith, and this officer receives a special congratulatory message from the G. O. C. for his excellent score.

LIEUT.-COL. RICHARD WOOD
1907-1911.

The Commandant (Lieut.-Col. A. J. M. MacLaughlin) was the first of the officers of the Corps to gain distinction by being mentioned in despatches in the Manipur Campaign, and on March 17th of this year he becomes the first officer in the Surma Valley Light Horse to be granted the Volunteer Officers' Decoration, and further on the 29th of July he was appointed as Honorary Aide-de-Camp to His Excellency the Commander-in-Chief in India.

There are two notices of the Provincial Medal in this report, for in addition to Lieut. Meredith above, Troop-Sergt.-Major H. M. Girling also wins it.

Further honours are gained by the Corps in that, on the disbandment of Lumsden's Horse, two members were granted Honorary rank in the Army :—Major H. Chamney, C.M.G., and Captain C. L. Sidey.

On 15th November, Captain S. A. Cooke, 1st Central India Horse, assumed the office of Adjutant vacated by Captain A. C. H. Smithett.

In connection with the Coronation Durbar at Delhi, fourteen members of the Corps under the command of Captain W. Mason left for Delhi on the 16th December. Apart from the escort provided for the Viceroy at Dacca, mentioned in a previous chapter, this was the first occasion when the Regiment had provided a detachment for a great public function. This occurred on 1st January, 1903.

Still further progress is reported for 1903. " The general drill shows improvement. I am glad to see that Manœuvring and Dismounted Service duties in the presence of an imaginary enemy has been extensively practised and that competitions under service conditions have been keenly contested."

The Regiment was inspected by Major-General Sir A. J. F. Reid, K.C.B., who expressed himself highly pleased with all he saw in camp, especially the keenness displayed, the willingness to endure hardship, and the amount of trouble taken by members in training both themselves and their horses under great difficulties. The Field Day, he said, was most instructive, and the men took cover and acted in every way as if the enemy were using ball and not blank ammunition. During the Camp, the Inspecting Officer unveiled the Obelisk erected by the members of the Corps to the memory of Colonel Eden Showers, who was killed in South Africa.

Honours and decorations now begin to fall thickly on members of the Corps. On 1st January, Captain Robert Heriot Henderson is decorated with a Companionship of the Indian Empire, on the 27th November, Lieut.-Col. W. R. Walker becomes the second officer to wear the Volunteer Officers' Decoration, and Lieutenant A. H. A. Meredith again wins the Provincial Medal for shooting.

In 1904 the Regiment was inspected by Colonel H. N. McRae, C.B., and there is a discussion about messing charges. "The expenses of the Camp for messing, Rs. 6/- per diem, appeared to me to be excessive, and must keep some men away. When Troops or sections assembled for drill, it is usually at some Officer's house, where a luncheon, of no mean order, is hospitably provided. This must mean heavy expense; some refreshment is necessary, but the scale should be very greatly reduced, and I think that some assistance might be given to Officers and Non-Commissioned Officers so circumstanced," reports the Inspector-General of Volunteers in India. This matter is referred to the Chief Commissioner of Assam, who forwards it to the Commandant. If anything happened as a result, there is no record of it in the Annual Reports.

The Lieut.-General Commanding the Forces, Bengal, makes one comment only on the Corps—a few words but full of praise —" A useful and efficient Corps."

In June, 1904, the Right Wing was called out for duty to disarm the detachment of Military Police in Silchar who had mutinied, and took over the Quarter Guard, Magazine, and Arms. The Corps was cordially thanked for the manner in which they had performed this rather unpleasant duty. The Chief Commissioner of Assam wired his thanks " for prompt assistance rendered at sacrifice of personal convenience." The G. O. C. Assam District also wired :—" The work for which the Volunteers were recently called out at Silchar has been satisfactorily carried out. Colonel McRae thanks all concerned for their prompt and admirable services," and the Deputy Commissioner, Cachar, wrote as follows :—

"To the Officer Commanding, S. V. L. H.
Dated, Silchar, the 16th June, 1904.

Sir,

"I have the honour to request that you will be so good as to convey to the Officers and Men under your Command who assisted in the disarmament of the Silchar Military Police Battalion, my cordial thanks for their prompt action on that occasion. I knew well how inconvenient it was for them to be absent from their employment at this the busiest time of the year. Their ready response to the call of duty, the tact and good temper with which they performed a rather unpleasant duty, and their cheerful acceptance of considerable personal discomfort, were most admirable. They have the satisfaction of knowing that they performed an important service to the State."

I have the honor to be,
Sir,
Your most obedient servant,
(Sd.) W. M. Kennedy,
Offg. Deputy Commissioner,
Cachar."

On the 8th June, Lieut. L. E. Dening, 33rd Light Cavalry, was appointed to succeed Captain Cooke as Adjutant, and on the 15th July, it is recorded that the Provincial Medal has again come to the Surma Valley Light Horse, the winner this time being Trooper A. Lumsdaine.

The Camp of 1905 was a record one as regards numbers, there being 177 on the Inspection Parade. Colonel McRae again inspected the Regiment and commented on the great improvement on the previous year. Lieut. A. H. A. Meredith refuses to allow the Provincial Medal to leave the Regiment by winning it again, this time under new conditions. These conditions are not mentioned in the Report but as the score is far lower than any others recorded it must be assumed that they were more difficult. The Adjutant, Lieut. Dening, was promoted to be Captain and shortly afterwards was appointed to be Aide-de-Camp to His Excellency the Governor of Bengal, and so resigned his office. He was succeeded by Captain A. G. Crocker, 22nd Cavalry. The Rev. W. Drew, Chaplain of the Regiment also resigned his commission this year.

The Corps was inspected during the Camp of 1906 by Lieut.-Col. L. C. H. Stainforth, Commanding the 3rd Brahmans, and again by the Inspector-General of Volunteers in India, Major-General J. Stratford Collins, but apart from the fact that they express themselves well pleased with what they saw there is no record of their reports.

On the 2nd May the Rev. W. E. White, who for many years had been a trooper in the Regiment was appointed to succeed the Rev. W. Drew as Chaplain.

More honours come the way of the Surma Valley Light Horse. Lieut. Meredith again wins the Provincial Medal; the "Playfair Cup," presented by Sir Patrick Playfair, Kt., C.I.E., for competition among Volunteer Corps having an efficient mounted detachment of not less than a troop (36 of all ranks), which was instituted for the first time in 1906, was won, and the Volunteer Officers' Decoration was awarded to Captain F. G. Loch, and Major A. R. Rich.

The Surma Valley Light Horse, as such, attained its majority in 1907, and it had become a definite part of the life of the Valley. The years following the South African war seem to manifest a great deal more keenness, and at this period it can look back on a history which had contained honourable service in two campaigns, and had been exceedingly useful to the State in other ways. All through this period the Commandants report steady increase in numbers and efficiency each year, and the reports of the Inspecting Officers show that the Government of India regarded the Regiment as a very

LIEUT.-COL. W. R. WALKER
SECOND IN COMMAND AND SOMETIME
ACTING-COMMANDANT 1908.

useful force. This year there was no inspection during Camp as by some mistake the Inspecting Officer, Major-General A. Pearson, Inspector-General of Volunteers, arrived two days after the Camp broke up, so that only a very few members of the Corps were on parade. Another honour was added to the record of the Regiment in that Lieutenant H. M. Girling won the Eastern Command Medal. It is believed that this was the only occasion when this medal came to the Province of Assam. Trooper Lumsdaine again brought the Provincial Medal to the Corps, and, to add to the record of this year, Lieut.-Col. A. J. M. MacLaughlin was appointed to be a Companion of the Indian Empire on the 28th June.

The Camp of 1908 was inspected by Brigadier-General E. H. Molesworth, G. O. C. Brigade, and his remarks were as follows:—

1. "The horses do not appear to be as good as last year, there being one or two undersized ones. On the whole, however, they were of a good stamp.
2. The led-horse work, though much improved, is still slow.
3. It is important to impress on officers and non-commissioned officers the advantage of keeping well away from their men at drill and of issuing their orders in a sharp and clear way.

The above are the only adverse criticisms that the General Officer Commanding has made, and has submitted a satisfactory report."

The Adjutant, Major A. G. Crocker, resigned and was succeeded for a short time by Lieut. G. Henderson, of the 38th Prince of Wales' Own Central India Horse, and on the 14th December Captain L. C. L. Bayley, 6th King Edward's Own Cavalry was appointed as Adjutant.

In March, Cavalry Training was substituted for Mounted Infantry Training and this change was greatly appreciated and considerably more interest was taken in the drill. The standard of qualification for marksmen was raised and a far higher efficiency was required from Volunteer units. Two officers were awarded the Volunteer Officers' Decoration, Lieut.-Col. R. Wood and Captain Walter Mason, while Sergeant L. W. Warner added his name to the winners of the Provincial Medal.

During the Camp of 1909 Lieut.-Col. A. J. M. MacLaughlin resigned his command and he was succeeded by Lieut.-Col. R. Wood. The attendance at Camp was far higher than in former years, nearly 200 being present. Two Inspecting Officers came down—Brig.-General H. Bower, C.B., Commanding Assam Brigade, and Major-General W. Du. Gray, C.B., Inspector-General of Volunteers, and the latter " verbally expressed his satisfaction at what he saw, " says the Annual Report. Later his terse report is " An efficient and very useful Corps. "

Sergeant L. W. Warner won the Provincial Medal for the second year in succession, and the following officers were awarded the Volunteer Officers' Decoration :—

Major A. J. Lamb, Major J. G. Knowles, and Captain R. St. J. Hickman.

Though there is no means of judging the numbers that attended the Camp of 1910—from the Commandant's remarks it must have been greater than ever. "The attendance at Camp," he writes, " from the very first day was a most acceptable improvement. Not only officers, but the rank and file were encouraged to give keener attention to their drill when they knew that their ranks would not be upset by late arrivals; as time for drills at Camp is very limited this early attendance must be much appreciated by all those who have the welfare of the Corps at heart and intelligibly understand its existence. It will be most gratifying to all to see this early and steady attendance continued at future Camps. The discipline which is of such importance to true soldiering was excellent."

The Camp was attended by the Commandant and Adjutant of the Assam Valley Light Horse—Colonel Jessop and Lieut. Hutchinson, and also by Surgeon-Captain Hewan of the same Regiment. The Commandant hoped that this would be the beginning of an exchange of visits, and two officers of the Surma Valley Light Horse attended the Camp of Exercise at Tezpur. General Bower again inspected the Regiment and expressed his satisfaction with the keenness and good fellowship which existed among the officers and men. His report was headed " General Efficiency and Fitness for Service " and went on to say — " A very useful Corps, well fitted for service and in every way equal to the part it might have to play in internal defence. " Sergeant L. W. Warner won the Provincial Medal for the third time in succession, and after this year the medal disappears from the Corps Records. It came to the Surma Valley Light Horse with such uncanny regularity that one can only assume that it ceased to exist. In May, King Edward VII died and was succeeded by H. M. King George V.

On the 7th December, Lieut.-Col. Wood, the Commandant, became ill and handed over the command of the Corps to Lieut.-Col. J. G. Knowles. On the 7th February, 1911, Colonel Wood died at Lungla, and in a Special Order Colonel Knowles writes—"It is with the very deepest regret, which will be shared by all ranks, that the Officiating Commandant announces the death on the 7th February, 1911, of Lieut.-Col. Richard Wood, V. D., Commandant of the Corps.

" Colonel Wood joined the Corps, then the Cachar Mounted Rifles in 1884, received his first commission in 1895 ; and was appointed Commandant in February, 1909, in which appointment he had previously officiated.

" He was heart and soul interested in all that concerned the welfare and efficiency of the Corps, and was loved and respected by all ranks. His services to the Corps were simply invaluable, and his death creates a void which it will be difficult to fill. All who knew him will mourn his loss, not only as their Commandant, but as a true and sincere friend. "

On the 8th February Lieut.-Col. J. G. Knowles was appointed as Commandant of the Surma Valley Light Horse. The Regiment furnished a contingent for the Coronation Durbar at Delhi under

Lieut. W. Townsend Smith, and another in connection with the King-Emperor's visit to Calcutta under Captain H. B. Fox, and was also represented at the Coronation procession in London by Major B. W. Hallifax. During Camp the Corps was inspected by Lieut.-Col. E. G. R. Wilkins, 114th Mahrattas, the Officiating Officer Commanding Assam Brigade. The Volunteer Officer's Decoration was awarded to Lieut.-Col. H. J. Mounsey and Captain W. Mackintosh, and early in 1912 Colonel Knowles was appointed to be Honorary Aide-de-Camp to his Excellency the Governor of Eastern Bengal and Assam. In that year also the Volunteer Officers' Decoration was awarded to Lieut.-Col. C. L. Sidey, Captain R. T. Fraser, and Lieut. A. H. A. Meredith, and further, in January 1913 Colonel Knowles received a Companionship of the Indian Empire, so honours and awards continued to flow into the Corps. The Camp of 1913 was attended by Sir Archdale Earle, the Honorary Colonel of the Corps, and Chief Commissioner of Assam, and the Regiment was inspected by Lieut.-Col. W. Mac L. Campbell, Commanding the 2nd Black Watch, who was greatly interested in all the sports and competitions. On the 1st of March the Right Wing paraded at Ramnagar for an inspection by Brig.-General K. E. Lean, Inspector-General of Volunteers, and field-firing operations were carried out. The Inspecting Officer afterwards called attention to some faults, the chief one being the failure of the firing line to pass on orders. "Members must bear this in mind in future. It is impossible to control a long extended firing line without passing words of command!" comments the Commandant.

On the 8th June, 1913 more honours come the way of the Commandant, for in addition to being A.D.C. to the Lieutenant-Governor of Eastern Bengal and Assam, he is appointed as Honorary Aide-de-Camp to His Excellency the Viceroy and Governor-General of India, and is granted the honorary rank of Colonel on appointment.

The Rev. R. T. Jourdain was appointed as additional Chaplain to the Regiment on the 2nd of June, and Major B. W. Hallifax was granted the Volunteer Officers' Decoration on November 14th.

LIEUT.-COL. J. G. KNOWLES, C.I.E.
1911-1919.

In 1914 the Regiment was armed with the short rifle and the old pattern carbine was withdrawn. Complaints had been made by Commanding Officers of the condition of the carbines, and though the shooting was of a very high standard, it would have been considerably better had the material the men had to shoot with been better. The immediate result was that there was no comparison with the excellent scores of previous years, but once the members became used to the new weapon an efficiency was established that has been maintained ever since.

In this year a "Charger Fund" was established to enable members to borrow a sum of money to purchase a pony. This Fund was ably supported by the Tea Agency Houses in Calcutta, and young members joining the regiment are able to buy a pony very quickly by a loan from the fund, repayable by instalments and not bearing interest.

The Camp report is still good and the Inspecting Officers—Brig.-General K. E. Lean and Brig.-General C. T. M. Crozier, Captain H. M. Girling, and Lieut. W. Townsend Smith Kavanagh—report favourably on the Regiment. During 1914 the Volunteer Officers' Decoration was awarded to Major H. M. Crozier, Captain H. M. Girling, Lieut. W. Townsend Smith, Lieut. J. E. Aird, and Lieut. E. Todd Naylor. During this year Captain Bayley resigned his office as Adjutant and was succeeded by Captain A. C. Norman, 5th Cavalry. The Sirocco Cup was won for the Regiment by Corporal Allan Simmonds, the first time for many years that the Cup had found a resting place in the Surma Valley.

With the outbreak of the Great War on 4th August, 1914, an increased interest appeared in every department, and the strength of the Regiment jumped up to 425. The Surma Valley Light Horse immediately placed its services at the disposal of the Government of India for active service, but though the offer was appreciated, it could not be accepted. An effort was then made to form a complete Regiment from all the Light Horse Corps in India, but this again was unsuccessful. Twenty-one members joined the Indian

Army Reserve of Officers, and many who were on leave joined units in Great Britain, and we see in Regimental Orders frequent notices to the effect that a member of the Surma Valley Light Horse was granted leave for " three years or for the duration of the war. "

Though there were excellent reasons why the Regiment as such, or a detachment from it, could not serve in the Great War, the matter was to be regretted. In the two campaigns where such a detachment had been permitted to serve—the Manipur Campaign and the South African War—the Regiment had acquitted itself honourably and there was every reason to suppose that this would have occurred again. But as it was, the men were scattered, and were found in every unit serving in the Great War and by their conduct and decorations brought glory to their old Regiment.

CHAPTER VII.

THE END OF THE VOLUNTEERS.
1915—1917.

THIS short chapter will cover the period from the beginning of 1915 until the 1st April, 1917, when the Surma Valley Light Horse ceased to exist as a purely Volunteer Regiment and became a unit of the Indian Defence Force. The volunteering days passed away with great regrets, and there are many members at present serving with the Corps who claim that the "old days were far better." Be that as it may, under war conditions the ordinary kind of volunteering could not go on. Internal Defence had to be reckoned with and Army Headquarters were bound to have a far bigger hold on the men than they could claim under purely Volunteer conditions. Whether the same conditions prevail to-day is not for us to judge, but the Surma Valley Light Horse can no longer claim to be a Volunteer unit. Its members receive allowances from Government and are compelled to perform a certain number of days of training.

The effect of the war was quickly seen in the keenness displayed by those who were not able to serve outside India. Musketry shows a great improvement in spite of the fact that no ammunition was allowed for practice, and the shortage of munitions is shown by the fact that the Commandant has to urge the necessity of collecting empty cartridge cases. Co-operation was established with the Military Police and the Assam Police and throughout the cold weather of 1914-15 there were frequent field days and night operations. Lieut.-Col. A. C. Ralph, 11th Rajputs, inspected the Regiment on the 4th of February, and Brigadier-General K. E. Lean saw the Right Wing in Silchar on the 3rd March. "In his speech after the inspection," reads the Annual Report, "he expressed himself as highly pleased at the steadiness and silence of the ranks during the Squadron and

Dismounted Action drills which formed part of the morning's operations." The Volunteer Officers' Decoration was awarded to Vet.-Lieut. J. Purves, Major H. B. Fox, Captain H. D. Marshall, and the Rev. W. E. White, during this year.

All through this year, leave is being granted to members of the Corps to join the various units in the field, and among them is the Adjutant, Captain A. C. Norman, who leaves on the 26th May. Then news began to come through of casualties and the first was Trooper Rennie, who had become Second-Lieutenant in the Indian Army Reserve of Officers, and was attached to the 25th Cavalry F. F., and died on the 2nd June; and on the 23rd September, Trooper E. A. Meldrum, while serving as Second-Lieutenant with the 2/8th Gurkha Rifles, was killed in action in France. Captain D. MacWhirter, of the Surma Valley Light Horse, was appointed to succeed Captain Norman as Adjutant on 27th November.

In 1916 there is a similar story, and the Surma Valley Light Horse is preparing itself for emergencies. Throughout the cold weather of 1915-16 Troop Route Marches were instituted for the first time and proved most instructive, and the Commandant reports that sixty-four members have joined various units, while the applications of several who had offered themselves for service with the Indian Army Reserve of Officers were under consideration. Farr.-Sergt. G. W. Muirhead, who was serving as Second-Lieutenant with the Indian Army Reserve of Officers, died of wounds on the 1st July, and Trooper H. Mears, serving as Lieut. in the I. A. R. O. was a prisoner-of-war in Turkey in October. During that year Captain W. K. Green was awarded the Volunteer Officers' Decoration, and the Rev. W. E. MacFarlane, who had been appointed Chaplain the previous year, resigned and went on active service.

In the cold weather of 1916-17 three camps were held—at Lungla in December, at Silchar in January, and the usual Camp of Exercise at Silchar in February, and the latter was inspected by

LIEUT.-COL. R. ST. J. HICKMAN, C.I.E.
1919 1924

THE END OF THE VOLUNTEERS 1915—1917

Brigadier-General R. G. Strange. Field operations were held in conjunction with the Armed Civil Police at each Camp, but the Commandant makes practically no comment on the work. He notes that seventy-three members are serving with the colours.

On 9th January, Trooper W. J. Arbuthnot, who was attached to the 53rd Sikhs as Second-Lieutenant, was killed in action in Mesopotamia; on the 15th March, Reservist J. E. Tait, who was serving in the Motor Boat Service in Mesopotamia, died on active service, and—the date is not given in the Records—Lance-Sergt. H. W. Hamilton was also killed in action.

The Adjutant, Captain MacWhirter, left for a Cavalry Regiment in France and Captain E. E. Dyball was appointed to succeed him.

The 31st March saw the end of the Surma Valley Light Horse as a Volunteer Corps and on the following day it became a unit of the Indian Defence Force, and to the regret of many members who had given their services freely and faithfully for a number of years, the conditions laid down for the new compulsory force prevented them from remaining as members. In order to comply with the new regulations it became necessary to drill during the rains, and the Surma Valley Light Horse, spread as it is over a vast area, with very bad roads and insufficient inter-communications, probably suffered more than any other Corps in India.

CHAPTER VIII.

THE INDIAN DEFENCE FORCE.

AS a unit of the Indian Defence Force certain "obligations" were demanded from the members of the Surma Valley Light Horse. There were two classes of members :—

1. Officers, soldiers and cadets who were between the ages of 16 and 41.

2. Officers and soldiers who were between the ages of 41 and 50.

The first group were required to perform 160 drills annually, including 18 for attendance in Camp; have six complete and continuous days in Camp, and pass an annual course of musketry. The second had to perform 70 drills only, and fulfil the other conditions.

The result was, during the rains of 1917, troop and section drills had to be performed in accordance with the I. D. F. regulations, and the Commandant noted that when he toured the District in the next cold weather he saw a tremendous improvement in drill of all kinds, but more especially in foot drill and rifle exercises. The Camp of Exercise which had previously lasted six days was now increased to fourteen, to enable every member of the Corps to comply with the rule that enacted that every man must attend Camp for six continuous days. Drills were more frequent and of longer duration than in previous years. Instructional parades were held in the afternoon and lectures on military subjects were given in the evenings, and on the whole the Camps were far more of a "military business" than they had been before. Brigadier-General R. G. Strange inspected the Regiment during Camp (1918), but there is no record of his report.

Here it might be mentioned that the Annual Report changes its character. Up to that of 1916-17 it had contained extracts from Regimental Orders, and these have proved to be exceedingly useful to the historian. From that of 1917-18 these Orders disappeared and the task of sifting material has become far more difficult, as the Annual Reports are the only sources of information.

Classes of Instruction are now held for officers, and the first of these lasted from 4th March—11th, and an examination followed this. Although this took place soon after Camp, every officer in the Regiment, except two who were taking a similar course in Calcutta, attended and all passed. As a result they were granted temporary commissions in the Army.

At the beginning of 1918 there were ninety-three members of the Corps on Active Service, and two other important events should be noted. The results of the 1917 Volunteer Cavalry Tent-Pegging Tournament are issued with those of 1918. The Surma Valley Light Horse was successful in each case, 1917 being the first year that the Tournament had been won by the Corps with a score of 48 points, which was improved upon in 1918 as the Regiment scored 51 points. A Regimental Polo Team was sent to Calcutta to compete for the Carmichael Cup. It succeeded in reaching the final, but was beaten by the Behar Light Horse by three goals to two. The team consisted of Captain Marshall, and Messrs. A. F. Stuart, C. N. W. Grimshaw and A. J. G. Cresswell. In July, 1918, there was a very serious earthquake in South Sylhet and a great deal of damage was done. The immediate result was that, of necessity, all drills in that part of the Surma Valley stopped, and a further result was that the Camp of 1919 was sparsely attended by members from that District. Also during 1918 we find the only record of a member of the Corps, as such, winning a decoration in the Great War. Lieut. G. G. Hills, who after seventeen years' service, joined the Army at the very beginning of the War, was awarded the Military Cross. *The London Gazette* of 26th September, 1918, contains the following report :— "During an advance his platoon came under very heavy machine gun cross-fire and was unable to advance or retire. Hills got the survivors back to the top of the hill which was then counter-attacked by the enemy, who advanced under an extremely heavy machine gun barrage to within 25 yards. With great gallantry and steadiness Hills beat off the attack with Lewis guns and bombs. The enemy then tried to capture the hill by coming in on his flank and was again beaten back. Owing to this Officer's courage and example the hill was retained."

Other decorations awarded during the year were a Companionship of the Indian Empire to Lieut-Col. W. Mason, and the Volunteer Officers' Decoration to Captain D. MacWhirter and Captain F. H. Carslaw.

On 11th November, 1918, the Armistice was signed and it is recorded that over one hundred members of the Corps were then serving with the Armies in the field.

The Camp of 1919 was held in Silchar from 3rd February—8th, and considering that it was a purely voluntary one and, as stated above, the earthquake of the previous July prevented the Sylhet members from attending, it was quite well attended, and further, the Surma Valley Light Horse was the only Light Horse Corps in the Brigade to hold a Regimental Camp that year. General Strange arrived on the morning of the 7th and proceeded to Ramnagar, where he first inspected the Regiment and then divided it into three units, each of which carried out a tactical scheme with ball ammunition. After this the General keenly criticised the day's work.

On the 28th February, Colonel J. G. Knowles resigned his command of the Regiment and with tragic suddenness died the following day. Colonel Knowles had been a member of the Corps almost since its inception and had served in the Manipur Campaign. It was he who commanded the Regiment in the last days of its existence as a volunteer unit, and was responsible for it during the early days as part of the Indian Defence Corps. The whole Regiment mourned his loss, feeling that they had lost a most efficient Commanding Officer and a sympathetic friend.

In April, 1918, notice was received in "B" Troop area that Kuki raids had taken place at Balladhun and Ainacherra and

LIEUT.-COL. H. D. MARSHALL, C.I.E., O.B.E.
1924-1927

assistance was urgently needed to prevent the raid extending further into Cachar. Twenty-four members of "B" Troop immediately turned out and undoubtedly saved further trouble. Many of the members travelled long distances and remained under arms for fourteen days until relieved by a detachment of the Assam Rifles. Here again the Surma Valley Light Horse proved its usefulness, for, had the Regiment not been in existence, there would certainly have been damage to property with probable loss of life.

The Regiment's services in 1918 received special commendation from the Chief Commissioner of Assam, who conveyed his appreciation " of the prompt and ready way in which your Corps rendered assistance to the Civil Authorities during the recent Kuki Raid in the North Cachar Hills. "

The " Kuki trouble " had begun earlier. At the end of 1917, an effort was made to recruit the Kukis for the Labour Corps in France. Unlike the Nagas and other tribes who knew from former expeditions what such enlistment meant, these Kukis of whom really very little was known, declined to serve. Two Kuki chiefs sent a message to Imphal in the Manipur State to the effect that their men were not going to leave their hills, and if we used force to compel our wishes they would use force against us. A few petty raids occurred during the hot weather and in September a detachment of the 4th Assam Rifles was sent to punish the offending chiefs. One village was burnt and then Captain Coote, who was in command of the detachment, received orders to return. This was a distinct mistake and at the end of 1917 the Kukis were raiding Manipur and had blocked the roads to Silchar and Burma, burning down the rest houses and murdering the *chowkidars*.

In late January 1919 two columns marched into the hills, and with one of these some officers of the Surma Valley Light Horse served:—Major H. B. Fox (who had just returned from France), Major H. D. Marshall, Captain Rees, and Messrs. J. E. Needham, G. D. Walker and L. R. Mawson. As a result of their services Major Marshall and Messrs. G. D. Walker and J. E.

Needham were mentioned in despatches, and Major Marshall was also awarded the Order of the British Empire, and Mr. Walker the Membership of the British Empire.

During this time Lieut.-Col. R. St. John Hickman had succeeded to the command of the Regiment, and a Regimental Polo Team was again sent to Calcutta for the Carmichael Cup consisting of Messrs. Grimshaw, Cresswell, T. G. Rawson and W. B. R. McWha, but here again success did not follow the team.

After the strain of the last four years, members of the Corps allowed their interest to flag and the season of 1919-20 appears to be one of the worst on record. There were reasons for this. Matters were in a state of flux and as all leave from India had been stopped during the war, opportunities were now seized for furlough. Also the members who had served on the various fronts during the War were returning to their gardens, and there was a further cause—a feeling that the Defence Corps was soon to cease to exist, and that a new Force—to be known as the Auxiliary Force, India, was to come into being.

Camp was poorly attended and also suffered from exceedingly bad weather conditions, and on the day of the Field Operations at Ramnagar, the Inspecting Officer (General Younghusband) and his Staff frequently had to get out and push their car, which over and over again stuck in the mud.

In 1920 the position of the Surma Valley Light Horse in the Army of India changed once more. The Indian Defence Force was disbanded and a new Auxiliary Force on a semi-volunteer basis was formed. This entailed a great deal of work, as the re-organisation of the Corps from a " compulsory unit " into a semi-volunteer unit could not be done without a great deal of anxious thought and careful consideration. In spite of the war weariness of the men who had served with the colours on every front where the British arms had fought, and the "fed up" feeling among those who had drilled with the Indian Defence Force, practically every man in the Surma Valley joined the new force. His Excellency the Viceroy,

Lord Chelmsford, visited Silchar in November, 1920, and inspected the Regiment. The officers entertained His Excellency at luncheon where he said " The Surma Valley Light Horse might be considered a pattern to all Corps in India for the loyal manner in which every man in the District had joined."

CHAPTER IX

THE AUXILIARY FORCE INDIA.

1921—1929.

THE year 1921 seems to mark a period of recovery from "war weariness." The Camp of that year was very well attended and was inspected by Major-General T. Cubitt, G. O. C., Presidency and Assam. The organisation of the corps was slightly changed and now consisted of three squadrons with four troops each and twelve Hotchkiss guns were also provided. The regiment was also re-armed, the 1914 pattern rifles being replaced by the S.M.L.E. Mk I.

That year the Volunteer Cavalry Tent-Pegging Tournament was again won, after a tie for the first place with the Behar Light Horse, each with a score of 46 points. At the run-off the Surma Valley Light Horse won by one point —43 to 42

In August, the Governor of Assam, Sir William Marris, arrived in Silchar and the corps formed a mounted escort for him. During his visit he unveiled a tablet which had been erected in St. Andrew's Church, Silchar, in memory of the men of the Regiment who had died on service during the Great War. The tablet contains the following names:—

Sergeant H. W. Hamilton	Died of Wounds, France.
Pte. R. S. Gamble	Killed in Action, France.
Farr-Sergt. G. W. Muirhead	Killed in Mesopotamia.
Pte. W. J. Arbuthnot	Killed in Mesopotamia.
Reservist E. J. Tait	Killed in Mesopotamia.
Pte. E. A. Meldrum	Killed in Action, France.
Pte. H. J. Andrews	Killed in Tochi Valley. (Afghan War)
Pte. D. Rennie.	Died of Enteric Fever.

On 3rd November, the Commandant, Lieut.-Col. R. St. J. Hickman, was appointed to be an Honorary Aide-de-Camp to

LIEUT.-COL. J. MACKNIGHT
1927-1930.

His Excellency the Viceroy and Governor General of India, and on the 1st, Major C. A. M. Paske, 23rd Cavalry, had succeeded Captain Dyball as Adjutant.

The Camp of 1922 was a successful one in every respect. General Cubitt was again the inspecting officer and expressed himself pleased with what he saw, with one exception, the carelessness of a number of men with regard to their rifles. Sir William Marris, Governor of Assam, visited Silchar on the last day of Camp, but was unable to see the regiment at work.

In January the Commandant had been decorated with a Companionship of the Indian Empire.

Major-General Cubitt was the inspecting officer again in the Camp of 1923 and he informed the Commandant that he saw a very great improvement. He was especially pleased with the appearance of the horses which in every way showed a great stride forward. Major Paske reverted to regimental duty in March and no successor was appointed until October, when Captain G. M. Stroud, of the 14th P. W. O. Scinde Horse, became Adjutant.

The 1924 Camp was inspected by Lieut.-Col. H. P. Yates, South Wales Borderers, and showed a great advance on the number attending and the work done. In November, Colonel R. St. J. Hickman, the Commandant, resigned and was succeeded by Lieut.-Col. H. D. Marshall.

During the Camp of 1925 a War Memorial Window to the men who had fallen in the Great War was unveiled by Mr. J. E. Webster, C.S.I., C.I.E., Commissioner of the Surma Valley, and dedicated by the Lord Bishop of Assam (Rt. Rev. G. C. Hubback), who was attended by the Rev. W. H. S. Wood, M. C., the Rev. W. E. White, and the Rev. T. W. Reese. The General Officer Commanding, Eastern Command, Lieut.-Gen. Sir G. de S. Barrow, was present at the ceremony. Before the unveiling Mr. Webster said:—

" This window which I am about to unveil has been erected to the Glory of God and in memory of the men of the Surma Valley Light

Horse who volunteered for Active Service in the Great War and died in the service of their Country. It has been subscribed for by generous sympathisers. His Excellency Sir John Kerr desires me to say that he esteemed it an honour to be invited to unveil this Memorial and much regrets that the pressure of public business has prevented him from doing so. In his absence I am here on behalf of the Government to do honour to the gallant men who gave their lives for us. Let me recall their names to you. Sergeant Hamilton, Farrier-Sergeant Muirhead, Privates Gamble, Arbuthnot, Meldrum, Tate, Andrews and Rennie. Their comrades who knew them and the cause for which they died need no memorial to keep their memory bright; but we hope that this Window will stand through many generations to be a witness and a sign that the men of the Surma Valley Light Horse were faithful to the motto of their Corps even unto death, and that we remembered their sacrifice. I therefore, unveil this Window to the Glory of God and in Memory of the Members of the Surma Valley Light Horse who died for us."

Towards the end of Camp, the G. O. C., Presidency and Assam District, Major-General Sir W. M. Thomson, arrived and inspected the Regiment. A notable change was seen in the arrangements for Camp. In the past, a considerable amount of time had been spent on the parade ground, but under instructions from Headquarters all this was altered. Tactical schemes and field operations, which included bridge-building and fording rivers, formed the major part of the work, and the interest in camp increased greatly. Another innovation was the establishment of a permanent riding school in Silchar with a staff of riding boys, and this, coupled with a still further innovation, a Horse Show, made for a great improvement in the horses of the Regiment. Further changes were made in the conditions of the Regimental Competitions and the individual element was subordinated to that of the Troop or Half Squadron. For this purpose an Aggregate Half-Squadron Trophy was instituted, points being awarded on team scores in each and every competition.

There was no inspection in the Camp of 1926, General Ward being unable to come, but the attendance was greater than for some years, there being an average of 149 men in Camp daily. The Permanent Staff had been sadly depleted and there were only three Instructors against the usual complement of six. Consequently work suffered somewhat, and the Presidency and Assam District were asked to do their utmost to keep this very important section of the Corps up to strength. The 1927 Camp again provided an innovation, for a Weapon Training Circus from the Prince of Wales Own Volunteers gave instruction and demonstration in the use of arms, and also inaugurated morning Physical Training which proved to be intensely popular. General Ward was present in camp for a short time, and Colonel Rowlandson, Deputy Director of Auxiliary and Territorial Forces, India, inspected the Regiment.

Lieut-Col. Marshall, who had been appointed an Honorary Aide-de-Camp to H. E. The Viceroy and had also received a Companionship of the Indian Empire the previous year, resigned in July, 1927, and was succeeded by Lieut.-Col. J. Macknight, who was appointed Honorary A. D. C. to His Excellency the Governor of Assam.

In order to further Regimental Polo a Surma Valley Light Horse Polo Club was formed. The main object was to purchase better ponies, and a system was instituted by which the club bought a certain number of ponies each year, which were drawn for, first by squadrons, then by troops and lastly by individual members. The result was that a far better class of polo pony appeared in the Valley and the standard of play became higher. Also the old Regimental Institute which had been used mainly by the Instructional Staff was turned into the Surma Valley Light Horse Club and the Commandant became President, with a Committee consisting of the Adjutant, Chaplain and Regimental Sergeant-Major, as ex-officio members, and one member from the Instructional Staff and one member from each Squadron. This has proved to be a boon to the younger members of the Regiment who might not be able to afford to join the larger clubs in the Station, and the ' regular tennis day '—Thursday—is always well attended. Captain G. M. Stroud returned to his Regiment and was succeeded in the Adjutancy by Captain W. E. D. Robinson, M. C., of the same Regiment, in September.

In November a Course of Instruction was held and was attended by a Weapon Training Circus from the North Staffordshire Regiment, and in the Camp of 1928 a Demonstration Platoon from the 52nd (Oxford and Bucks) Light Infantry gave instruction on how, and how not, to do various things. In the absence of the G. O. C. Presidency and Assam District, Colonel C. D. Roe, Commanding the 2/8th Gurkha Rifles, inspected the Regiment, and Major A. E. Maitland from the Eastern Command, and Major N. G. R. Coats from Army Headquarters, also attended.

In October, General Sir John Shea, G. O. C., Eastern Command, arrived to inspect the Regiment. During the previous week over twenty inches of rain had fallen, and the roads became almost impassable. This did not deter the Corps from putting up an excellent show, and special credit was due to " C " Squadron, some of whom had to ride twenty miles, and then box their own horses before getting to the train to complete the journey to Silchar. Sir John Shea was entertained to luncheon by the Regiment and said that he had always desired to see the Surma Valley Light Horse, and now having seen them, and realised that they were ready to overcome any difficulties that might be placed in their way, he could safely leave this part of the country in their hands.

The Camp of Exercise in 1929 was shortened to six full working days and this resulted in greater concentration. " We got through a very full programme of work, and thanks to excellent staff work, we had no slack time. I am glad to say that there were very few dismounted men, a distinct improvement on the last year or so. Discipline and keenness throughout the Camp were remarkably good Members attending the Camp were as follows:- Officers 15

LIEUT.-COL. A. B. BEDDOW
1930

Other Ranks 214..." writes Colonel Macknight in the Annual Report of 1928-29.

Major-General H. D. O. Ward, C.B., C.M.G., G.O.C. Presidency and Assam District, inspected the Regiment and assisted in judging the Lord Curzon Shield Competition and the Inter-Squadron Field Firing Competition.

The changed conditions of modern cavalry warfare created another innovation and towards the end of this year three Mobile Machine Gun Sections, with machine guns mounted on lorries were formed, one for each Squadron.

The Regiment entered a team for the Calcutta Polo Tournament in December, 1929, and played in both the Carmichael and Ezra Cup Competitions. The younger members of the Regiment were chosen, mainly with an idea of competing regularly for these Competitions and giving them an idea of faster polo than can be obtained in the Surma Valley. The team was:— Captain W. E. D. Robinson, M. C. (Adjutant) and Messrs H. A. Davey, R. B. Scott, and T. A. Allan. Considering that the team had no combined practice it played remarkably well, and after a very bad beating by the Government House team in the Carmichael Cup, it then improved with each game and defeated the 60th Rifles and the 13th Lancers in the Ezra Cup, succumbing to the Crusaders in the third round. The Calcutta newspapers paid a great tribute to the team and one wrote:—" The Surma Valley Light Horse did some amazing things. Until they arrived in Calcutta they had not played together as a team." They were defeated, according to the same paper, by the Crusaders because a number of their ponies were injured, and in that match could only call upon six. But the mere fact that they entered and put up such a remarkably good performance points to a great future in competitive polo.

CHAPTER X.

THE FIFTIETH YEAR, 1930.

AFTER the wonderful record of the Regiment it was fitting that the presentation of its Colours should coincide with its Jubilee Year.

These Colours, a Guidon, were presented to the Regiment by H. M. The King-Emperor George V., and it had been previously arranged that His Excellency The Viceroy (Lord Irwin) should hand them over in January, 1929. His Excellency's visit to Assam had to be cancelled, and though another effort had been made to obtain His Excellency Sir E. L. L. Hammond, the Governor of Assam, for this purpose on Armistice Day, November 11th, 1929, this again failed.

On February 11th, 1930, during the Camp of Exercise, Major-General H. E. ap Rhys Price, the General Officer Commanding the Presidency and Assam Districts, performed the ceremony, which had been very carefully rehearsed on the previous day. The Regiment was drawn up in a hollow square, mounted, and the Guidon, escorted by Major A. B. Beddow and Lieut. C. W. N. Grimshaw, was brought to where the Rt.-Rev. G. C. Hubback, D.D., the Lord Bishop of Assam, was standing, who was attended by the Rt.-Rev. Richard Thomas, D.D., the Lord Bishop of Willochra, South Australia, and the Rev. W. H. S. Wood, M.C., Chaplain of the Regiment, and the Bishop consecrated the Guidon.

After the Consecration the Guidon was handed by Major Beddow, to Major-General H. E. ap Rhys Price who then presented it to Lieut.-Col. J. Macknight, who received it on bended knee. After the presentation the General addressed the Regiment. "Lieut.-Col. Macknight, Officers, N.C.O's and Men of the Surma Valley Light Horse:—I feel it a great honour that I have been invited to-day to present this Guidon to your Regiment which is now nearly completing its fiftieth year since it was first raised. Formed originally on the 22nd October, 1880, as the Sylhet Volunteer Rifle Corps, you combined in 1884 with the Cachar Mounted Rifles, that were

CONSECRATION OF THE GUIDON.   FEBRUARY 1930

PRESENTATION OF THE GUIDON.   FEBRUARY 1930

raised after you, to form the Cachar and Sylhet Mounted Rifles, which title was changed in August 1886, to your present title of the Surma Valley Light Horse. Your unit has been represented in several expeditions by individuals or detachments, notably in the Manipur Expedition of 1891, and the South African War, when " B " Company of Lumsden's Horse was largely of your unit. In the Great War some thirty per cent. of the Corps represented it in various parts of the Empire, while the balance maintained law and order in India. Since then you served in the Kuki Expedition of 1919, and I feel sure that your unit is ready for further service whenever and wherever it may be necessary.

" Thanks to a succession of good Commanding Officers, a good Staff, and the willing co-operation of members, the unit has always maintained a high reputation. Its skill in shooting is well-known and you have won the Provincial Medal for shooting twice as many times as all other competitors, and, as I saw for myself in the recent tournament in Calcutta, your horsemanship and skill in polo was highly thought of.

" To such a unit it is, therefore, a great pleasure to present a Guidon, an emblem that was first introduced into the British Army about the Fifteenth Century and was borne by a guide or leader of horse. Hence its name. That pleasure is enhanced by the admiration a Regular has for those who do voluntary military service and by their influence maintain the Pax Britannicum in large tracts of the Empire. These Guidons were borne before a regiment and it was considered a disgrace to let them fall into an enemy's hands, hence they are symbolical of the honour of a regiment which followed them and fought for them to the death.

" In entrusting this Guidon to your care I feel that I am handing it over to a unit whose past history and high standard will ensure that it is borne by those who will ever be foremost and lead the way in the path of duty and action on behalf of King and Country."

After the address the Commandant handed the Guidon to the Standard Bearer, Squadron-Sergt.-Major H. St. J. Morrison, and the Regiment, preceded by the Colours, marched past the G. O. C. in review order, first at the walk, then at the trot and finally at the gallop, every movement being well executed, and the Guidon, escorted by a Squadron, was carried to Headquarters. That evening for the first time, the Guidon was hung in Mess.

Thus ended a landmark in the history of the Surma Valley Light Horse.

The Camp itself was exceedingly well attended and the numbers created a record for any Camp outside the compulsory camps during the Great War. Field operations were held with the 1st Assam Rifles and the judges decided that the result was a draw, the Surma Valley Light Horse being successful in the first part of the operations and the 1st Assam Rifles in the second. All the competitions were keenly contested, so keenly that they were praised by the Adjutant, that most critical of regimental officers. On the last night of Camp, Lieut.-Col. Macknight announced the resignation of his command as he was retiring from India, and the Regiment presented him with a rose bowl in token of their esteem. Also the Adjutant, Captain W. E. D. Robinson, M.C., announced that he had been appointed to the Auxiliary Force Headquarters Staff in Calcutta, and was leaving the Corps at the end of March. Colonel Macknight was succeeded by Lieut.-Col. A. B. Beddow, and on the 5th of April, Captain B. W. G. Walker, M.C., of Prince Albert Victor's Own Cavalry (11th Frontier Force) assumed the duties of Adjutant.

During the whole of the history of the Regiment, many N. C. O's and men received the Volunteer Long Service Medal, but as the records are incomplete, it was thought to be invidious to mention those whose names have occasionally appeared in the Annual Reports, and so it happens that only those decorations that have been awarded to officers have been noted; but the fact that the highest decoration that can be gained by a soldier in peace time was awarded to Regt-Sergt.-Major Albert Edward Cass cannot be passed over. In Indian Army Orders dated the 28th March, 1930, it was

Officers, Surma Valley Light Horse, 1930
With Major General H. E. ap Rhys Price, G. O. C.
Presidency and Assam.

announced that His Excellency the Commander-in-Chief had been pleased to award the Meritorious Service Medal to Mr. Cass and with it the annuity of £5, the award being antedated to the 6th September, 1929. Mr. Cass joined the Army in 1900 and after seeing service in the South African War and in the Great War he was placed on the Indian Unattached List for service with Volunteer Regiments. He had considerable experience in this direction before he came to the Surma Valley Light Horse as Regimental Sergeant Major in 1920, and proved himself a very able Warrant Officer.

Just before the Manipur Campaign an Inspecting Officer was prophetic and said that the Regiment would be exceedingly useful if it were needed. Forty years later, when presenting the Guidon, the General Officer Commanding, Presidency and Assam District, uttered words that again proved prophetic. He said that he was entrusting the Guidon to a Regiment that "will ever be foremost and lead the way in the path of duty and action on behalf of King and Country," and within two months the Surma Valley Light Horse took the opportunity to fulfil these words.

Before entering on a description of these events, another curious fact should be noted, and it is that this history finishes very much as it began. The first chapter mentioned that several planters, though, of course, there was no Regiment in existence in those days, volunteered their services for the Indian Mutiny in 1857 and did good work in Cachar when the mutineers from Chittagong entered that district.

On 19th April, 1930, a cipher telegram was received at Headquarters from Presidency and Assam District Command ordering the mobilisation of one squadron to proceed immediately to Chittagong, for on the previous day a raid by one hundred Bengali members of the "Republican Army" had been made on the Auxiliary Force and Police Armouries, and seven men, including the Sergeant Major of the Assam Bengal Railway Battalion, had been murdered. This attack had been very carefully planned. Every man had his task specified and their watches had been synchronized with London time and the exact variations worked out. At 9-30 p.m. on 18th April, the operator at the Telephone Exchange was held up with a revolver and chloroformed, and the Exchange burnt. Almost simultaneously a party went in cars to the Assam-Bengal Railway Battalion Armoury and the leader of the rebels was disguised as the Adjutant of that unit. He walked up to the sentry and demanded the key of the Armoury. On being told that the Sergeant Major had it, he immediately shot this sentry and also two others, and when Sergt-Major Farrell came out on hearing the firing he was shot as well. Then using crowbars and by tying a rope to a car the Armoury was forced, all the rifles and revolvers taken, and after saturating the place with petrol the building was set on fire.

The rebels then dashed to the Police Armoury where again the sentry was murdered and the arms taken. From the operation plans that were discovered later, their ultimate aim was to murder all the Europeans in Chittagong, and actually a number of the rebels went to the Club for this purpose, but by a fortunate chance everybody had gone home and the place was in darkness. In the meantime the plans of the rebels were frustrated by a British Sergeant who dashed off to an Armoury in the Assam Bengal Railway Workshops and got a Lewis gun which he brought into action and disabled three cars full of the captured rifles and revolvers. It is almost certain that this fact and also that the rebels were not aware that there existed this small armoury, saved the situation. The rebels then escaped into the jungles near Chittagong.

In the meantime, another party had derailed a ballast train at Dhoom, a few miles out of Chittagong, their intention being to hinder the arrival of reinforcements, and yet another party cut the telegraph wires. One fact escaped their notice. The ships in the port are fitted with wireless and it was by this means that the news of the raid was made known to Calcutta.

Shortly after the arrival of the first telegram noted above, a second was received by Corps Headquarters which stated that the

Detachment at Chittagong, 1930.

position was well in hand and that only one Troop was needed. By 3 p.m. on the 19th, orders were issued for the necessary concentration and at once despatched by motor cyclists to all Troop leaders in "A" and "B" Squadrons detailing the number of men required, so that they should equally be distributed over the Cachar area. In the short time available it was not possible to mobilize men from "C" Squadron. The details were passed on by hand to each member of the Corps called out so that in no case was the telegraph used.

At 10 a.m. on Sunday morning (20th April) and four hours earlier than was expected, the Troop mustered in Silchar. The men called out for duty were:—Major A. B. Beddow, Captain W. B. R. McWha, Lieut. T. A. Blacklaws, S.-S.-M. C. J. Shorey, Corporal T. W. L'Estrange, Lance-Corporals H. J. Caple, J. A. S. Reid, J. Rogers, and T. W. Sheppard, Troopers C. C. M. Bayley, C. H. Blacker, A. H. Burnett, T. Edmond, C. P. Hollis, F. M. Howard, T. B. R. Honeyman, D. D. Iliff, E. R. Ludlow, R. J. H. MacGeagh, H. McArthur, J. G. McIntosh, J. L. McIntosh, J. S. Mercer, C. W. Mountain, H. Millett, C. D. Marshall, J. R. Masson, W. Morrison, R. M. Paterson, K. Pooley, W. T. Sturrock, H. T. Street, J. S. R. Telfer, W. Williamson, T. Wylie, and A. J. Young. The detachment was under the command of Captain W. B. R. McWha, and the late Adjutant, Captain W. E. D. Robinson, M. C., accompanied the Troop as liason officer. They entrained at 4 p.m. and arrived at Chittagong on the morning of the 21st, where they found that one hundred men of the Eastern Frontier Rifles under Colonel Dallas Smith had arrived on the previous morning and were scouring the hills for the rebels. The Surma Valley Light Horse was then made responsible for the safety of the town, and a series of motor patrols was inaugurated. This entailed some hardship as it meant that each man had only one night off in four. They were responsible for a double guard at the petrol dump, where it was thought the rebels might attack again, and the motor patrols went on ceaselessly during the night.

On the 22nd, the rebels were located in the jungles about five miles from Chittagong and at 4-30 p.m. the detachment, with a force of Eastern Frontier Rifles, were dashed to the scene in motor cars. The exact position of the enemy was vague, but on approaching a hill where it was thought the rebels might be, the Eastern Frontier Rifles were thrown out on the flanks and the Surma Valley Light Horse proceeded to hold the front. On nearing the hill a man opened fire on the advancing troops with a revolver, and immediately this was followed up by constant fire from the hill top. Fortunately for the Surma Valley Light Horse there was a small *nullah* near by, but with the enemy only one hundred and fifty yards away and, apparently, well supplied with ammunition, the position might have been serious. Had the rebels been able to shoot with any degree of accuracy we must have had a large number of casualties. As it was there was only one, a trooper being slightly wounded by a bullet grazing his arm.

In their haste to get away the tripod of the Hotchkiss gun was left behind and Trooper Iliff did a smart piece of work, in that, lying on his back in the *nullah* which contained a foot of water, he held the gun over his face while another trooper fired it.

One party under Corporal L'Estrange went out on the right flank and there did some excellent sniping. Trooper Baylay, the son of a former adjutant of the Regiment, also did good work and managed to get within thirty yards of the enemy and caused a great deal of damage. For this he was mentioned in the despatches of Captain H. R. Taitt, M.C., Adjutant of the Assam Bengal Railway Battalion who commanded the action. Captain Robinson also behaved with characteristic gallantry and by his example under fire encouraged the remainder of the troop.

Firing was kept up until dusk. It was not then known that the whole of the rebels were on the hill top, and it was presumed that only thirty were there, and as the Surma Valley Light Horse was responsible for the safety of Chittagong they were recalled from the action and immediately took over the patrol work. The Eastern

Surma Valley Light Horse Camp, 1930

Frontier Rifles remained at the position but later on they were withdrawn as well. The following morning a party with a machine gun raked the position but getting no response they approached the hill and found nine dead and two mortally wounded, while the ground was thickly covered with empty cartridge cases, giving some idea of the amount of ammunition the rebels had at their disposal. In addition to the casualties mentioned, it is certain that others were wounded, but actual figures could not be obtained.

Two days later six members of the troop were called out to round up an armed rebel, who had been discovered in a house in the bazar. He took cover in a culvert and had two revolvers. He fired one shot which nearly got S.-S.-M. Shorey, and then he himself was killed.

On the 26th they were relieved by the 3rd Battalion of the Assam Rifles and left Chittagong on the 27th.

So, once again the Regiment had proved its usefulness, and on this occasion, owing to the fact that it reached Chittagong so quickly after the raid, it undoubtedly prevented the situation from becoming more serious.

The purpose of this book is now completed and the history of the Surma Valley Light Horse has been traced through fifty years. In all its phases it has received the loyal support of those who have served in its ranks, and no Regiment has ever had better material. From the Commandant down to the newest joined trooper there has always been manifested a large amount of enthusiasm, and the various successes that have fallen to its lot are to be attributed to the loyalty, keenness, and enthusiasm which have been displayed throughout its history.

A large measure of its success is due to the Regular Army Officers and N. C. O's.—the Adjutants and the Staff Sergeant Instructors—who have been attached to the Corps. The long list in the Appendix shows that almost every regular Cavalry Regiment that has served in India has sent men to help in the training of the Surma Valley Light Horse. These men have not only caught the spirit of the

Regiment but have helped to develop its enthusiasm, and have assisted in building up one of the finest volunteer Cavalry Regiments in India. This is no mere boast; this history is an attempt to prove the point, for every honour open to Volunteer and Auxiliary Force Regiments has found a resting place with the Surma Valley Light Horse, and the tradition of the Regiment is bound up with its motto :—

NON SIBI SED PATRIAE.

APPENDIX I.

Roll of Officers who have served with the Regiment.

Honorary Colonels.

Sir Charles Elliott	... 1883-1887	Sir L. Hare	... 1906-1909
Mr. D. Fitzpatrick	... 1887-1889	Sir Archdale Earle	... 1909-1911
The Hon'ble J. W. Quinton	... 1890-1891	Sir N. D. Beatson-Bell	... 1912-1918
Sir W. E. Ward	... 1891-1896	Sir W. S. Marris	... 1918-1922
Sir H. J. S. Cotton	... 1897-1902	Sir John Kerr	... 1922-1927
Sir J. B. Fuller	... 1902-1909	Sir E. L. L. Hammond	... 1927

Commandants.

Lieut.-Col. J. Knox-Wight	1883-1887	Lieut.-Col. R. St. J. Hickman	... 1919-1924
Lieut.-Col. A. Milne	... 1887-1895	Lieut.-Col. H. D. Marshall, O.B.E.	... 1924-1927
Lieut.-Col. E. C. Showers	... 1895-1899	Lieut.-Col. J. Macknight	... 1927-1930
Lieut.-Col. A. J. M. MacLaughlin	... 1900-1907	Lieut.-Col. A. B. Beddow	... 1930
Lieut.-Col. R. Wood	... 1907-1911		
Lieut.-Col. J. G. Knowles	1911-1919		

Lieutenant-Colonels (*with date of appointment.*)

Theodore D'Orville Partridge	... 1895	Harold John Mounsey	... 1909
Alfred Allan	... 1895	Charles Lyon Sidey	... 1911
William Renny Walker	... 1900	Walter Mason	... 1915

Majors.

O. Sheffield	... 1885	Benjamin William Hallifax	... 1911
J. W. S. Dalrymple Clark	... 1895	Henry Montgomery Crozier	... 1912
Henry Chamney, C.M.G.	... 1899	Henry Benedict Fox	... 1915
Alexander James Lamb	... 1899	Robert Thomson Frazer	... 1920
Henry Alexander Brown-Constable	... 1900	Harry Morton Girling	... 1920
Arthur Frederick Rich	... 1900	Edward Banham Baker	... 1920
Francis Gisbourne Loch	... 1907		

APPENDIX

Captains.

S. D. Jackson	...	1883
Alexander Stewart	...	1884
James Kerr	...	1885
Donald Ferguson	...	1885
M. J. Balfour	...	1886
G. F. Playfair	...	1887
Ernest Livermore	...	1887
H. W. Morris	...	1887
W. Meldrum	...	1887
R. Thomson	...	1892
Reginald Steward	...	1893
Charles Samuel Walliker	...	1893
Charles Macalister Thomson	...	1894
Henry McBain	...	1898
William Mackintosh	...	1909
Edward Byers Moir-Byers	...	1910
Alexander Mason Mackessack	...	1911
William Kersling Green	...	1912
John Findlay Wilson	...	1912
Roderick Rees	...	1913
Dudley Macwhirter	...	1915
Frank Henderson Carslaw	...	1915
Frank Pullen	...	1920
Ralph Mortimore	...	1920
Phillip Stanley Doubell	...	1924
Roland Adair Palmer	...	1927
David Esmond Gomme	...	1928
Arthur Kerrison Preston	...	1928
William Barry Ritchie McWha	...	1929

Lieutenants.

D. A. Laing	...	1883
J. O. Bowhill	...	1883
Arthur Odling	...	1884
Henry Weir	...	1888
E. Bulteel	...	1885
Robert Heriot Henderson	...	1885
Peter McElroy	...	1885
A. Abel	...	1885
G. C. A. Kentish	...	1886
E. L. Edgar	...	1887
D. Taylor	...	1887
Henry Carleton Sproull	...	1888
J. C. Grant	...	1888
Frederick Charles Henniker	...	1893
Arthur Henry Templer	...	1896
Henry Ross Blakeney		1896
Arthur Lea-Juckes	...	1896
David Lamb Black	...	1896
Gerald Edward Pierson Thesiger	...	1899
Sidney George Hart	...	1900
Arthur Henry Austin Meredith		1900
William Taylor Cathcart	...	1900
John Henry Montague Stevenson	...	1907
Walter Reginald Winder	...	1910
Charles MacLeod	...	1912
William Townsend Smith	...	1913
Harold Lowther Bigge	...	1915
Herbert Mark James	...	1915
Reginald George Boyle	...	1915
Harry Gilbert	...	1916
Peter MacIver	...	1917
Robert Pringle	...	1920
Thomas Walter Green	...	1920
Tom Murdoch Odling	...	1921
John Armstrong Elliott	...	1923
Christopher Roland Fox	...	1923
Cyril Nicholas Wrigley Grimshaw	...	1924
James Walker Macbeth Watson	...	1929

APPENDIX

Second-Lieutenants.

R. G. H. Carew	...	1888	James Erskine Aird ...	1905
G. W. Peter ...	...	1890	Francis Joseph Jeffries ...	1909
T. S. Mulligan ...	...	1891	Louis William Warner ...	1915
G. A. Wilson ...	...	1892	Alisdair Francis Stuart ...	1917
Henry William Moore	...	1893	Thomas Cundy Neems ...	1927
William Duncan Stewart	...	1895	Harold Edward Bennett ...	1927
James Purves ...	...	1896	Thomas Edward Holbrook ...	1927
William James Reid	...	1897	John Crabtree Henderson ...	1928
Harvey Sanderson	...	1897	Tom Alexander Blacklaws ...	1929
Edward Acheson Chartres	...	1899	Victor Knott	1929
Charles William Adam Trevor		1900	William Gerald Grinley ...	1929
Samuel John Best	...	1904	George Edward Bates ...	1929
George Campbell Balfour	...	1904		

APPENDIX II.

Roll of Staff.

Adjutants.

Lieut. Ernest Livermore (acting) ... 1883-1885	Captain L. C. L. Bayley ... 1908-1913
Captain M.S.C. Hatton ... 1885-1888	Captain A. C. Norman ... 1913-1915
Captain G. F. Willes ... 1888-1893	Captain D. Macwhirter ... 1915-1917
Captain H. M. Johnston ... 1893-1897	Captain E. E. Dyball ... 1917-1921
	Major C. A. M. Paske ... 1921-1923
Captain A. C. H. Smithett 1897-1902	Captain G. M. Stroud ... 1923-1927
Captain S. A. Cooke ... 1902-1904	Captain W. E. D. Robinson M. C. ... 1927-1930
Lieut. Lewis Dening ... 1904-1905	Captain, B. W. G. Walker, M. C. ... 1930
Major A. G. Crocker ... 1905-1908	

Medical Officers.

A. J. M. MacLaughlin ... 1884	James Harloe Christopher Thompson ... 1913
J. S. Reed ... 1885	John Dunlop ... 1914
J. C. Dundee ... 1886	William Roy MacDonald ... 1914
P. B. Le Franc ... 1887	Charles Girdleston Terrell ... 1921
Samuel Arthur Powell ... 1895	Cecil Cantilupe Harrison ... 1921
George Clark ... 1898	Donald Meek ... 1921
Ronald Thomas Graveley ... 1902	James Stewart ... 1921
Charles Edward Sylvester ... 1904	James Joseph Moriarty ... 1922
Henry Alexander ... 1905	Rolf Creasy ... 1929
Reginald Anthony Murphy ... 1912	

Chaplains.

Rev. T. T. Crossfield ... 1884	Rev. W. E. MacFarlane ... 1914
Rev. W. Drew ... 1893	Rev. H. W. H. Ainsworth ... 1920
Rev. W. E. White ... 1905	Rev. W. H. S. Wood, M.C. ... 1922
Rev. R. T. Jourdain ... 1913	

APPENDIX III.

INSTRUCTIONAL STAFF.
Regimental-Sergeant-Majors.

J. M. Robertson	1885	W. G. Burgess	1909
F. G. Loch	1886	T. H. Hounsell	1911
A. H. Templer	1890	W. Bebbington	1917
R. J. Easterbrook	1894	A. E. Cass	1920
J. W. Woodward	1901		

Regimental Quartermaster Sergeants.

D. MacLeod	1884	J. W. Leather	1915
C. S. W. Hopkins	1891	J. C. Martins	1919
D. Ferguson	1905	T. W. Hickey, D.C.M.	1920
J. Purves	1910	B. C. Brooks	1922
A. Lumsdaine	1913	A. E. M. Smith	1925

Staff Sergeant Instructors with Regiment and date of appointment.

R. Leigh	14th Hussars	1883
S. Roberts	9th Lancers	1884
A. Kearney	14th Hussars	1884
W. Haste	12th Lancers	1885
A. Lawrence	17th Lancers	1885
R. Slater	14th Hussars	1885
D. McCarthy	2nd Dragoon Guards	1886
W. McGill	1st Dragoon Guards	1887
J. T. G. Bell	8th Hussars	1889
J. B. Thomas	2nd Dragoon Guards	1888
A. C. Chisholme	5th Lancers	1889
R. M. Strangeways	1st Dragoon Guards	1889
W. C. Welch	16th Lancers	1890
G. Reynolds	7th Dragoon Guards	1890
R. J. Easterbrook	5th Dragoon Guards	1894
M. Coyle	5th Lancers	1894
J. W. Woodward	5th Lancers	1894
T. Brennan	16th Lancers	1895
A. Tuley	18th Hussars	1897
J. W. Spindler	19th Hussars	1897

APPENDIX

F. Markwick	18th Hussars	1897
P. Kelly	5th Dragoon Guards	1898
F. R. A. Lightfoot	3rd Hussars	1898
G. Robinson	15th Hussars	1900
L. Kench	15th Hussars	1901
F. W. Malpass	15th Hussars	1903
T. H. Hounsell	15th Hussars	1904
S. J. Reimers	1st Dragoon Guards	1905
J. Walker	12th Lancers	1905
E. J. Timmis	13th Hussars	1906
A. T. Freeman	6th Dragoon Guards	1907
W. G. Burgess	The Carabiniers	1909
C. E. Mitchell	10th Hussars	1909
F. Imms	8th Hussars	1910
G. Jarmey	1st Dragoon Guards	1910
T. S. Millgate	14th Hussars	1911
A. Pope	1st Dragoon Guards	1911
J. Francis	14th Hussars	1912
B. Harrop	7th Dragoon Guards	1912
J. C. Martins	7th Hussars	1914
W. G. Walby	6th Dragoon Guards	1915
G. Simister	6th Dragoon Guards	1916
E. Langridge	7th Hussars	1917
W. Bebbington	1st Dragoon Guards	1917
C. Humphries	7th Hussars	1919
B. C. Brooks	7th Hussars	1920
A. E. Cass	4th Hussars	1920
T. W. Hickey, D.C.M.	21st Lancers	1920
C. Peel	11th Hussars	1922
R. C. Scarterfield	7th Hussars	1922
J. R. Burton	16th-15th Lancers	1923
R. C. Collingridge	11th Hussars	1924
A. E. M. Smith	4th-7th Dragoon Guards	1924
T. G. Robertson	The Royal Scots Greys	1925
F. G. Atwell	61st Field Battery, Royal Artillery	1926
H. E. Whalley	88th Field Battery, Royal Artillery	1926
P. D. Scrivener	4th Hussars	1927
A. Bell	3rd Hussars	1928
W. V. Brown	3rd Hussars	1928

APPENDIX IV.

DECORATIONS AND AWARDS GAINED BY MEMBERS OF THE CORPS.

Knight Companion of the Indian Empire

Sir Robert H. Henderson   Sir W. J. Reid.

Companion of the Star of India

Sir W. J. Reid   J. E. Webster.

Companion of the Order of St. Michael and St. George

Henry Chamney.

Companion of the Indian Empire

A. Milne.
A. J. M. MacLaughlin.
J. G. Knowles.
R. St. J. Hickman.
J. M. Hezlett.
W. Mason.
H. B. Fox.
H. D. Marshall.
J. E. Webster.
J. J. T. Macknight.

Order of the British Empire

H. D. Marshall.

Member of the Order of the British Empire

G. D. Walker.

Military Cross

N. F. Bacon.
R. N. R. Evans.
G. G. Hills.
A. G. Morris.
W. J. Robertson.
T. W. T. Street.
W. H. Tilbury.
W. H. S. Wood.

Distinguished Flying Cross

G. Mackrell.
H. C. Hawkins.
F. R. Johnson.

Distinguished Conduct Medal

J. G. Bartlett.

APPENDIX

Military Medal

A. Brown.
J. G. Bartlett.
J. Grant.
D. Hutchinson.
J. S. Munn.
A. E. Slade.

Foreign Decorations

J. G. Bartlett	Croix de Guerre (France.)
J. Grant.	Croix de Guerre (Belgium.)
W. G. Grinley	Croix de Guerre (France.)
F. W. W. McCrea	Croix de Guerre (France.)
S. de B Miller	Order of St. George (Russia.)
J. S. Munn	Medaille Militaire (France.)
R. A. Palmer	Croix de Guerre (France.)
W. H. Tilbury	Order of Leopold II (Belgium.)
W. H. S. Wood	Croix de Guerre (Belgium.)

Volunteer Officers Decoration

A. J. M. MacLaughlin.
W. R. Walker.
A. F. Rich.
F. G. Loch.
R. Wood.
A. J. Lamb.
W. Mason.
R. St. J. Hickman.
J. G. Knowles.
H. J. Mounsey.
C. L. Sidey.
W. Mackintosh.
R. T. Fraser.
A. H. A. Meredith.
B. W. Hallifax.
H. M. Crozier.
H M. Girling.
W. Townsend Smith.
J. E. Aird.
J. Purves.
H. B. Fox.
H. D. Marshall.
W. E. White.
W. K. Green.
J. Henderson.
D. Macwhirter.
F. H. Carslaw.
F. Pullen.
J. Macknight.
R. Mortimore.
P. S. Doubell.
A. B. Beddow.
E. B. Baker.
J. Dunlop.

Kaiser-I-Hind. Second Class
R. T. Fraser.

Meritorious Service Medal
Regt.-Sergt.-Major A. E. Cass.

APPENDIX

MENTIONED IN DESPATCHES
Manipur Campaign 1891
A. J. M. MacLaughlin.

South African War, 1899-1901

H. Chamney.
S. A. Powell.

C. L. Sidey.

Great War, 1914-1918

N. F. Bacon.
J. G. Bartlett.
A. Brown (twice.)
J. W. Hallan.
C. C. Harrison.
G. G. Hills.

R. A. Kerr (twice.)
T. Mannion.
H. St. J. Morrison.
R. A. Palmer.
W. H. Tilbury (twice.)
H. A. Willis.

Kuki Expedition 1919

H. D. Marshall.
J. E. Needham.
G. D. Walker.